O9-BSU-492

WILLIAM A. NOLEN, M.D.

THE BABY IN THE BOTTLE

An investigative review of the
Edelin case and its larger meanings for the
controversy over abortion reform

Coward, McCann & Geoghegan, Inc.   New York

CARNEGIE LIBRARY
LIVINGSTONE COLLEGE
SALISBURY. N. C. 28144

For permission to quote from copyrighted material, the author gratefully acknowledges the following: *The New England Journal of Medicine*, for an excerpt from "Deeper into Abortion," by Bernard M. Nathanson, M. D., reprinted by permission from *The New England Journal of Medicine*, Volume 291, Page 1189, 1974; *The New England Journal of Medicine*, for an excerpt from "The Edelin Fiasco," by F. J. Ingelfinger, M. D., reprinted by permission from *The New England Journal of Medicine*, Volume 292, Page 697, 1975; *National Review*, for an excerpt from "The Edelin Verdict, Part Three: The Cultural Context," March 14, 1975, reprinted from *National Review*, 150 E. 35 St., New York, N. Y. 10016; *The Boston Herald American*, for an excerpt from "Fairness and the Edelin Case," by Anthony LaCamera, copyright © 1975 by *The Boston Herald American*; *The Boston Herald American*, for an excerpt from "Is Jury System a Game of Chance," by Dave O'Brian, copyright © 1977 by *The Boston Herald American*; *The New Republic*, for an excerpt from an editorial by Michael Kinsley, copyright © 1977 by *The New Republic*, all rights reserved; Harper's Magazine Company, for an excerpt from "Why We Thought Dr. Edelin Was Guilty" in *Harper's Weekly*, March 14, 1975, copyright © 1975 by Harper's Magazine Company, all rights reserved; *The Los Angeles Times*, for an excerpt from "A Doctor Performing Legal Surgery Should Not Be Jailed," by Harriet Van Horne, copyright © 1975 by *Los Angeles Times*, reprinted by permission; The Non-Sectarian Committee for Life, for permission to reprint an advertisement entitled "A Noose Is Tightening Around Man & Civilization."

Copyright © 1978 by William A. Nolen, M.D.

All rights reserved. This book, or parts thereof, may not be reproduced in any form without permission in writing from the publisher. Published on the same day in Canada by Longman Canada Limited, Toronto.

Library of Congress Cataloging in Publication Data
Nolen, William A.
   The baby in the bottle.

   1. Edelin, Kenneth Carlton, 1939-   2. Trials (Infanticide) —Massachusetts—Boston.   3. Abortion—Law and Legislation —Massachusetts. I. Title.
KF224.E35N6   345'.73'0285   78–490
ISBN 0-698-10899-X
Printed in the United States of America

THE BABY IN THE BOTTLE

Books by WILLIAM A. NOLEN, M.D.

THE MAKING OF A SURGEON
A SURGEON'S WORLD
HEALING: A DOCTOR IN SEARCH OF A MIRACLE
SURGEON UNDER THE KNIFE
THE BABY IN THE BOTTLE

For younger readers
SPARE PARTS FOR THE HUMAN BODY

345.73
N791

To attorneys Newman Flanagan and William Homans
with thanks.

106886

Many people helped me obtain the information I needed to write *The Baby in the Bottle.* Some of them are named in the book. Others, for a variety of reasons, are not mentioned. I thank them all.

It is possible, even probable, that some of those who helped me will disagree strongly with what I have written. I take full responsibility for everything I have written. Readers who disagree with what I have said should direct their animosity toward me.

Using the Edelin case as a touchstone, Dr. Nolen traces liability beyond a single physician to our entire society and its ill-defined attitude toward abortion. Brilliantly reasoned and basically humane, THE BABY IN THE BOTTLE is destined to be widely discussed— and to influence radically the debate on abortion as it is practiced in America today.

WILLIAM A. NOLEN, M.D., is the author of the bestselling THE MAKING OF A SURGEON; A SURGEON'S WORLD; HEALING: A DOCTOR IN SEARCH OF A MIRACLE; and SURGEON UNDER THE KNIFE. Born in Holyoke, Massachusetts, a graduate of the College of the Holy Cross and Tufts Medical School, he spent his surgical internship and residency at Bellevue Hospital in New York City and then settled in Litchfield, Minnesota, where he is currently in practice. His articles have appeared in medical journals and leading American magazines, and his column appears monthly in *McCall's* magazine. Dr. Nolen was last year awarded the prestigious American Heart Association's Howard W. Blakeslee Award for Best Book. Dr. Nolen and his wife, Joan, have three sons and three daughters.

Jacket design by HONI WERNER
Portrait of the author rendered from photograph by ARDEN BURLEIGH

COWARD, McCANN
& GEOGHEGAN, INC.
Publishers
200 Madison Avenue
New York, N.Y. 10016

illiam Homans
ay, February 4,
nneth Edelin)

did you do after
?

I weighed the fe-
ner of formalde-

ereafter, sir, to

gy cutting room

he fetus, doctor,
the plastic con-
?
still in the surgi-

cal specimens.
he surgical con-
ou put the spec-

city of approxi-
quarts.
?
on.

hology department
Edelin performed
s a routine witness
ribed here were in
the hospital's pa-

THE BABY IN THE BOTTLE

Preface

The clerk: "Members of the jury; Hearken to an indictment. The Commonwealth of Massachusetts, Suffolk, SS, at the Superior Court begun and holden at the City of Boston and for the County of Suffolk for the transaction of criminal business on the First Monday of April in the year of Our Lord one thousand nine hundred and seventy-four, the jurors for the Commonwealth of Massachusetts on their oath present that Kenneth Edelin on the third day of October in the year of Our Lord one thousand nine hundred and seventy-three did assault and beat a certain person, to wit, a male child described to the said jurors as 'baby boy' and by such assault and beating did kill said person; a True Bill.

"To this indictment the defendant at the bar pleads not guilty and for trial places himself upon the Country, which Country you are.

"You are sworn to try the issues. If he is guilty, you shall say so.

9

William A. Nolen, M.D.

"If he is not guilty, you shall say so and no more.
"Members of the jury, hearken to the evidence."

So, officially, with this announcement of the clerk of the court on January 16, 1975, began what is now known as the Edelin case.

From late 1973, when it became apparent that Dr. Kenneth Edelin would, in all probability, be brought to trial for manslaughter, until December of 1976, when the Supreme Court of Massachusetts announced its final decision, the case was one which aroused, angered and divided not only the members of the medical and legal professions but the public at large.

Although technically Dr. Edelin was tried for manslaughter, the incident for which he was indicted was, in the opinion of most of the world, a matter of abortion. Dr. Edelin had performed an abortion on a young woman. Now he was being brought to trial for what he had done. Those who felt that a woman had a right to decide, with her doctor, what should or should not be done to her body felt strongly that Dr. Edelin was being unjustly persecuted. Those whose conviction it was that the life of the fetus in a woman's uterus deserves the protection of the law, regardless of the wishes of the woman, were convinced that if Dr. Edelin were not punished, a precedent would be set that would eventually lead to a total disregard of the sanctity of human life.

The members of the medical profession were as divided on the merits of the Edelin case as was the general public, with one rather major exception: although some doctors believed that Edelin had committed a crime and others believed he was innocent, most were worried that if he were convicted, it would represent one more intrusion of the legal profession into the work of doctors. Even those who felt that Edelin was guilty and should be convicted feared that conviction might lead to a situation in which every act of a doctor would be so

10

closely scrutinized by the public, and lawyers in particular, that doctors would lose the freedom to exercise their best judgment in those many situations where there is neither time nor opportunity to check the propriety of the act with any committee or court. Without freedom to act quickly and freely, as his conscience, judgment, education and experience dictated, much of the physician's power to help his patients would be gone.

At the time of the trial most of the major news magazines and many of the influential, intellectual magazines of opinion published articles and letters about the case. *Newsweek*, in its March 3, 1975, issue, put a picture of a sixteen-week-old fetus on the cover and ran a long story which dealt not only with the case but with the growth and development of a human being from the instant the sperm penetrates the ovum—the moment of conception—to the time, ordinarily 266 days later, when the child is born. I read most of the magazine and newspaper articles when they were published and again several times over the last two years, as I worked on this book. I think it is fair to say that though there were strong opinions expressed both for and against Edelin and the position he represented, the vast majority of Americans were simply deeply disturbed. More than anything else they wished that there was no Edelin case. They didn't want to examine abortion with all its moral implications, as the Edelin case was forcing them to do. They wanted the entire problem to shrivel up and blow away.

It seemed obvious to me then that the abortion "problem," despite our desires, was not going to go away. That opinion has been reinforced by those developments that have occurred, not only since the Edelin case, but ever since the Supreme Court decision in January of 1973 in the case of *Roe* v. *Wade*. It was that decision which liberalized abortion laws and made a case like the Edelin case not only a possibility but a probability. Now, in the United States, abortions are being performed at the rate of more than a million a year. In Wash-

ington, D.C., in 1976 there were more abortions performed than there were live births. In 1976, 25 percent of all pregnancies ended in abortion. The abortion problem is with us, and all the maneuvering we may do cannot prevent us from confronting it. Some of us will be forced to consider it when either we or a female friend or relative becomes pregnant with an unwanted child; those of us who practice medicine will probably have to deal with the problem many times in our professional lives. And even if we never personally have to deal with a specific abortion case, we are all going to be influenced by the liberalized abortion laws because of the way they change society. To offer only one example, before the liberalization of abortion, it was a relatively simple matter to adopt a child. Now there is a long list of couples waiting for children, and a black market in babies exists.

Since we cannot avoid the abortion problem, since it won't go away if we simply shut our eyes to it, then the only reasonable steps we can take, distressing as they may be, are those that lead us to as full a knowledge of the problem as we can possibly have.

When the Edelin case was legally over, it seemed to me that a reexamination of that case in a book where one could write freely, without all the restrictions necessary in a courtroom, could be of great value. In a courtroom one must sometimes refrain from presenting all the facts in order to preserve the legal prerogatives of either the prosecution or the defense. This is understandable. But though such restrictions lead to legal judgments, they may keep from us all the information we need if we are to achieve true understanding. I had followed the case closely as it was reported in the newspapers and could think of many questions that had not been asked and to which I would have liked answers. The case, since it was opening new ground and would undoubtedly establish legal precedents, was one that was, necessarily, treated gingerly by the judge and the lawyers for both prosecution and de-

fense. It seemed to me, even after its conclusion, a case from which we, the public, had not learned as much as we should have.

So I decided to go back over the case. I had met, casually, attorney William Homans who had acted as Dr. Edelin's chief counsel. Since I happened to be in Boston at the time, I had attended the hearing in April of 1976 when the Massachusetts Supreme Court had listened to the appeal by the defense to reverse the original verdict and the defense of that verdict by the prosecutor. Until then, those were my only direct contacts with the people involved in the case.

Since that time—April of 1976—I have read the 5,000-plus pages of the Edelin trial manuscript. I have interviewed, among others, defense attorney William Homans, prosecuting District Attorney Newman Flanagan, District Attorney Garrett Byrne, Special Assistant to the District Attorney Charles Dunn, Boston City Councilor Albert O'Neil, and dozens of physicians and nurses who were, in one way or another, involved in the case. I also spoke with Dr. Kenneth Edelin, who was friendly, treated me very courteously—even showing me around the gynecology service at Boston City Hospital and introducing me to the nurses who work there—but who preferred not to be interviewed by me in matters pertaining to the case. I have read other interviews he has granted.

I have read the legal appeal briefs of both the defense and the prosecution; the minutes of the grand jury hearing as a result of which Dr. Edelin was indicted; articles by doctors, lawyers and journalists on the case and matters related to it. Since I am writing this preface as I begin to write the book, it may be that I will refer to other sources of information as the book unfolds.

I have found the case both fascinating and informative. I hope the reader will agree.

1

The person who was responsible for setting in motion the legal machinery that resulted eventually in the trial of Kenneth Edelin, M.D., for manslaughter was Boston City Councilor Albert "Dapper" O'Neil.

The Boston City Council, composed of nine councilors elected at large, is the governmental organization responsible for running the city of Boston. The relationship between the mayor and the city council is like that between the president and the Congress, or a governor and the state legislature. The mayor can make all the proposals he or she likes, but it's the city council that allocates the money necessary to implement the programs. The mayor has prestige and a certain amount of power, but the city councilors are the people who actually run Boston.

The job is one that pays reasonably well—the annual salary is $20,000—but it hardly puts one in the "wealthy" class. In Boston in 1973, all but two of the city councilors were lawyers. Their law practices, presumably, flourished because

15

they had the political power that comes with the councilor's position. They could find jobs for their friends, fix parking or speeding tickets, get passes to the Celtics or Bruins games. They also decided what firms would be granted those contracts that didn't require sealed bids, automatically awarded to the low bidders. The job of city councilor, to which most councilors devoted only a small portion of their time, was a nice political plum—the kind of political job for which there was and is a lot of competition.

But Albert O'Neil was not and is not a typical Boston city councilor. Albert O'Neil, known throughout Boston, and indeed all of Massachusetts, as "Dapper," because of his flamboyant style of dress is a fifty-seven-year-old, silver-haired, ruddy-faced Irish bachelor who lives in a small house in Roslindale, one of the less affluent sections of Boston, with his married sister and her family. Dapper was a small-time contractor till 1971 when he decided to get out of the business and run for the city council. In Roslindale he had always been an active Democrat—you can hardly find an Irish Republican in Boston—and he was known as a great storyteller. When he ran for the city council, he ran hard, but he finished tenth in the field.

However, Louise Day Hicks, nationally known for her strident opposition to busing in Boston, had run both for Congress and for the city council. Originally she had planned to accept both positions if she won them both—which she did—but then thought better of it and decided not to accept her position on the council. This allowed Dapper to move up to the ninth position and take Ms. Hicks' place on the council. (After one term in Congress, Ms. Hicks was defeated for reelection. She is now back on the city council. She, like most of the others, is a lawyer.)

When Dapper O'Neil was elected to the city council, he decided, he told me, "to make it a full-time job." Which he did, with a vengeance. The poor and powerless of Boston—the

16

"little people"—quickly came to look upon Dapper as their champion. He was in his office in the new Boston City Hall all day, every day. When he wasn't in his office they could call him at his home. "Though I finally had to put a stop to that," he said. "Calls would come at two or three in the morning from drunks who wanted me to come down and get them out of jail. Having the phone ringing all the time wasn't fair to my sister. Now everyone knows I'll be in my office during the day, and most evenings I'm at some public function or a wake. They can talk to me then. But when I'm home, except for real emergencies, I expect the people to respect my privacy. I can always bail them out in the morning."

Dapper has an opinion on every matter and is not only willing but eager to voice it. He keeps a very close watch on everything that Mayor Kevin White does and loves to catch him at any activity that smells the least little bit of political chicanery. When he learned the mayor was converting one of the patrol boats that had been used by the police to control activities on the Charles River to a yacht that could be used by the mayor to entertain visiting dignitaries, Dapper had a field day. He raised so much hell over this "waste of the taxpayer's money" that the project was abandoned.

The media quickly learned to love Dapper. He was always good for a story. And to make certain the media didn't neglect him, Dapper got in the habit of sending out weekly news releases revealing any skullduggery he knew or suspected was going on in his city. He became a regular and very popular guest on one of Boston's morning radio talk shows, a show to which listeners could phone in when they had questions to ask or opinions they wanted to express. When Dapper was on the radio, the station switchboard was constantly lit up. He became so popular that, when I talked to him in February of 1977, he was preparing to take over as host for a week while the regular host went on vacation. If there is such a thing as a peculiarly Irish "gift for gab"—and there is—Dapper has it.

William A. Nolen, M.D.

In January of 1973, soon after the Supreme Court liberalized the abortion laws, the staff at Boston City Hospital began doing a great many abortions. It was, after all, the city hospital, the one to which the poor and indigent patients—most of them black or Puerto Rican—came when they needed medical care. Since, notoriously, it is the poor and indigent who most often find themselves with unwanted pregnancies, the marked increase in abortions at Boston City was not surprising.

To say that the increase in abortions at Boston City was understandable is not to say it was acceptable, particularly to the many Catholic nurses who worked there. The idea of abortion was repugnant to them; they had been raised, as have most Catholics, to look upon abortion as a mortal sin, one for which—whether you were the patient who underwent it, the doctor who performed it or the nurse who assisted at it—the penalty was eternal damnation. Nor, according to Church law, was it sufficient to avoid playing any active role in the abortion process. If you were a Catholic, you had a moral obligation to do what you could to prevent others from carrying out abortions. One way to do this was to write to City Councilor Dapper O'Neil and tell him what was going on at Boston City. A lot of people, not only the nurses who worked there but friends with whom the nurses discussed the situation, wrote to Dapper. Dapper was chairman of the Health and Hospital Committee of the city council. In fact, since he was the only councilor who worked at his job full-time, he was chairman of most of the city council committees. When the "abortion" letters started pouring in, Dapper decided he would look into the situation at Boston City and determine what, if anything, needed to be done.

2

As a preliminary to understanding the Edelin case, it is essential that we understand the Supreme Court decision in the case of *Roe* v. *Wade*, since it was that decision which indirectly led to the indictment of Kenneth Edelin.

The *Roe* v. *Wade* case originated in Texas when a pregnant single woman, referred to as "Roe," ("Roe" or "Doe" are the names courts routinely assign to people whose anonymity is to be protected) brought a class action challenging the constitutionality of the Texas criminal abortion laws, which proscribed procuring or attempting an abortion except on medical advice for the purpose of saving the mother's life. In the course of its long trail through the courts, a second case was linked to the Roe case. This second case was brought by the "Does," a childless married couple, the wife not being pregnant, basing alleged injury on the future possibilities of contraceptive-failure pregnancy, unpreparedness for parenthood and impairment of the wife's health. By the time the *Roe* v. *Wade* case had wended its way through all the primary and

appellate courts to the Supreme Court, the case constituted an attack on all state and local laws that prohibited or regulated abortion.

The *Roe* v. *Wade* decision, handed down by the Supreme Court on January 22, 1973, is, as is customary and probably a necessity in Supreme Court decisions, a long document replete with references to legal and historical precedents on which the justices, in part, based their decision. It contains, for example, an explanation of the historical derivation of the Hippocratic oath, which, in all of its various translations, contains the statement "I will neither give a deadly drug to anybody if asked for it, nor will I make a suggestion to this effect. Similarly I will not give to a woman an abortive remedy." (The Supreme Court decision refers to the work of the late medical historian Dr. Ludwig Edelstein, who concluded that even in Hippocrates' day the prohibition of abortion was subscribed to by only a small group of Greek philosophers; that, in fact, most Greek thinkers commended abortion, at least prior to fetal viability. The traditional Hippocratic oath is no longer taken by most new medical school graduates. An oath composed by the World Health Organization, one that does not contain any reference to abortion, is used instead.)

A short book could be devoted to the logic and references of the Roe-Wade decision. At other points in this book we will have to refer to some of them, but for the moment it is sufficient to quote the three paragraphs of the decision that are critical to the Edelin case:

(a) For the stage prior to approximately the end of the first trimester, the abortion decision and its effectuation must be left to the medical judgment of the pregnant woman's attending physician.

(b) For the stage subsequent to approximately the end of the first trimester, the State, in promoting its interest in the health of the mother, may, if it chooses, regulate

the abortion procedure in ways that are related to maternal health.

(c) For the stage subsequent to viability the State, in promoting its interest in the potentiality of human life, may, if it chooses, regulate and even proscribe abortion except where necessary, in appropriate medical judgment, for the preservation of the life or health of the mother.

Trimester means "three months" or ninety days. Since most normal pregnancies are 266 days in duration, it is convenient to refer to the stages of pregnancy in terms of trimesters.

As of January 22, 1973, Massachusetts—as well as all the other states—was in a position where all their laws prohibiting or regulating abortion were unconstitutional. Theoretically, a doctor could abort a woman up until the day she gave birth to the child. True the Supreme Court had given the state the right to regulate abortions during the second trimester (for example, by insisting they be performed in a hospital); and the Supreme Court had given the states the right, if they wished, to prohibit abortion entirely in the third trimester (except for cases where abortion was "necessary, in appropriate medical judgment, for the preservation of life or health of the mother"). But, until each state passed the laws it was permitted to pass to regulate abortions, it was, in effect, "open season" on abortions.

Massachusetts did not pass laws regulating abortion until August 2, 1974, so in Massachusetts this "open season" legally ran from January 22, 1973, till August 2, 1974. It was on October 3, 1973, while the "open season" was in effect, that Kenneth Edelin performed the abortion that led to a manslaughter indictment.

* * *

William A. Nolen, M.D.

The Supreme Court's decision in the case of *Roe* v. *Wade*, that women had a right to an abortion any time during the first six months of their pregnancy, struck a particularly hard blow to the state laws of Massachusetts.

Massachusetts has and deserves a reputation as a "puritan" state. Despite the existence since the late 1960s of an area in lower Washington Street known as the "Combat Zone"—an area where "dirty" movies, nude dancers and prostitutes abound—the people of Massachusetts have fought long, hard battles for what they conceive of as the sanctity of the home and of marriage. Even after the Second World War, which brought with it a definite loosening of the nation's moral climate, Boston went on banning books as innocuous—in retrospect—as *Forever Amber*. The city fathers were determined to protect their wives and daughters from the moral decay they were convinced was sweeping the country. In fact —difficult as it is to believe—until 1966 it was illegal in Massachusetts for a physician to give birth control information (other than instructions in the "rhythm system," also known as "Vatican roulette") even to married couples—a law which was, of course, impossible to enforce.

With the Supreme Court's decision, not only was Massachusetts' antiabortion law wiped off the books, but with it went related laws that prohibited the sale of drugs or articles to procure abortions and dissemination of information or advice about abortion. In other words, although New York State had had a liberalized abortion law since 1971, at the time of the 1973 Supreme Court decision it was, theoretically, still illegal for a physician practicing in Massachusetts to refer a patient who wanted an abortion to an abortion center in New York. It was even illegal for the Massachusetts physician to tell his patient that such abortion centers existed. These laws were, as might be expected, widely ignored.*

*However, in a case decided in 1969, the Massachusetts supreme court agreed that, despite the strict nature of its antiabortion law (in

22

But not by everyone. There are, not only in Massachusetts, but all across the United States, many physicians as well as lay people to whom the concept of abortion is completely repugnant. Many of these physicians are Catholics, but not, by a wide margin, all. Among those doctors who are strongly antiabortion one finds Protestants, Jews and atheists.

When the Supreme Court gave women the right to have abortions, there were six residents—doctors in training—on the obstetrical-gynecological staff at Boston City Hospital. At that time there were no full-time salaried doctors in the ob-gyn department. Dr. David Charles was the chief of the department, but, as is the case in many city hospitals, Dr. Charles devoted most of his time to the private practice at which he earned his living. The other fully trained, licensed obstetricians and gynecologists who worked at Boston City did so, like Dr. Charles, on a voluntary basis. They gave the interns and residents guidance and assistance when they needed it; they worked both in the outpatient department and on the hospital words, helping out as necessary; but their primary obligation was to their own private practices.

With the liberalized abortion law the work load of the six residents soared. They had all the work they needed before the change in the abortion law. Now, to the unrelenting regular flow of women to be followed through pregnancy and delivery and to the routine gynecological surgical schedule—D&Cs for diagnosis or treatment of spontaneous abortions, hysterectomies for any of a dozen or more reasons, Caesarian sections, operations to repair "fallen" bladders—were added the hundreds of patients who wanted their pregnancies terminated. The work load increased by about 50 percent.

Among the residents swamped with additonal work was Dr. Kenneth Edelin. Dr. Edelin was in his second year as a resi-

---

effect since 1845), a physician could perform an abortion in Massachusetts "in good faith and in an honest belief that it is necessary for the preservation of the life or health of the woman."

dent; one year of internship and three years of residency training are required before a physician is "board eligible," i.e., entitled to take the examination which, if he passes it, will certify him as a Diplomate of the American Board of Obstetrics and Gynecology. It is this certification which is required if you are to be classified as a specialist in your given field. (I, for example, am a Diplomate of the American Board of Surgery.)

Dr. Edelin was, at thirty-five, a few years older than his fellow residents. After receiving his bachelor of arts degree from Columbia University in 1961, he had taught high school math and science at the Stockbridge School in Stockbridge, Massachusetts, for two years. In 1963 he entered Meharry Medical College in Tennessee, graduating in 1967. After graduating from Meharry, he had taken a one-year rotating internship at the United States Air Force Hospital at Wright Patterson Air Force Base in Ohio. He was then assigned to the RAF Lake Heath Air Force Base in England as a captain and general medical officer in the American Hospital there. He spent three years at the base, dividing his time between general practice and the practice of obstetrics and gynecology.

When he was discharged from the Air Force in 1971 he applied to and was accepted as an obstetrics-gynecology resident at Boston City Hospital. With each year of training a resident is given increasing responsibility and, in his first year of residency, which ran from July 1, 1971, through June 30, 1972, he was allowed to perform uncomplicated deliveries and minor gynecological surgery without supervision, though he could, if he encountered any unanticipated complication, ask for help and either a senior resident or an attending physician would come to his aid. But Dr. Edelin had good judgment and rarely found that he needed any help in managing the patients assigned to his care. From July 1, 1972, to January 22nd, 1973, Dr. Edelin, as a second-year resident, spent most of his time doing gynecological surgery.

24

With the increased patient load that followed the Supreme Court decision, it was necessary to establish a routine in the outpatient department that would enable the doctors, nurses and aides to sort through the patients who wanted abortions and provide them not only with the proper surgical or medical care but with the most informed counseling that could be made available. No one who worked at Boston City had any desire to turn the place into an abortion mill. The doctors, nurses, aides and administrators all wanted to be certain that every woman who came there seeking an abortion knew the risks that were involved in the procedure and knew what other options were available to her before she chose—if she did choose—to have an abortion. And, of course, it was absolutely imperative that the doctor determine, as best he could, how advanced the pregnancy was. This was necessary not only because the technique to be used in performing the abortion depended on the stage of pregnancy, but because, after twenty-four weeks, it was theoretically possible that the child-fetus could survive outside the mother. So after this time the rights of the child-fetus to a chance to live had to be weighed against the mother's right to complete control over her own body. No one at Boston City Hospital wanted to get caught in the trap of aborting a viable fetus.

The screening process in the outpatient department was a relatively simple one. The woman who wanted an abortion would, after registering, talk with and be examined by a senior medical student and/or an intern. Boston City is closely associated with Boston University Medical School, which is just across the street from Boston City, and medical students from Boston University rotate through the hospital's various departments in the course of their medical training. If, after the doctor had examined and talked with her, he or she concluded that she was less than twenty-four weeks pregnant, and if she still wanted an abortion, she would be referred to one of the social workers who would explain to her all the oth-

25

er alternatives. The social workers, specially trained in this counseling, were black, white and Puerto Rican. For the Spanish-speaking patients, Spanish-speaking counselors were available.

The patient would be informed, for example, that if she chose to have the baby and keep it, she could. If she decided to have the baby and put it up for adoption, the hospital would make the arrangements. If she still insisted that she wanted an abortion, arrangements would be made to admit her to the hospital. Finally, before she could be admitted for any abortion, she would have to be examined by either a senior resident or an attending physician.

Some of the women who came to the hospital seeking abortions would, after the counseling, decide to have their babies. Most, however, had already considered the alternatives before coming to the hospital and so would elect to proceed with the abortion. One side effect of this sudden surge in abortions was that there was now in Boston a supply of fetuses which were the result of planned abortions. This led to a scientific study that was in turn to lead not only to the threatened prosecution (as yet unresolved) of three other doctors for a violation of a Boston statute known as the "grave-robber's law" but indirectly to the Edelin case.

3

One of the questions doctors must regularly answer in treating pregnant women for various complaints is "How will this treatment affect the fetus?" Generally, for example, particularly during the first three months of pregnancy, doctors will try to avoid taking any X rays of a pregnant woman for fear that the radiation, which in small doses is not harmful to the mother's adult tissues, might damage the immature, developing tissues of the fetus in her uterus.

When he prescribes medications for the pregnant woman, similar considerations arise. The fetus receives its nourishment through the placenta, the pancake-shaped organ attached to the inner wall of the uterus, which is in fact a network of blood vessels. Nutrients pass from the mother's bloodstream through the placenta along the veins in the umbilical cord to the fetus. Waste products from the fetus' body pass in a reverse direction; from the fetus along the umbilical arteries to the placenta and then into the mother's veins to be excreted through her lungs, kidneys or intestine.

William A. Nolen, M.D.

Until a few years ago physicians referred to the "placental barrier," a term now in less common use. However, while it was once believed that most of the medications a mother ate or had injected into her would not reach the fetus because they would be unable to get across the placenta, we now know that theory was wrong. For example a mother who is a heroin addict and who stays on heroin through her pregnancy will give birth to a baby who is a heroin addict. The child will become addicted while in the uterus and, if not given heroin or a substitute drug shortly after birth, will exhibit all the signs of heroin withdrawal.

We now suspect that almost everything a mother eats or has injected into her will, to some extent, pass the placental barrier. Some medications may pass rather freely so that the level of the drug in the infant's blood will be approximately the same as in the mother's. With other substances, probably because the molecules of the drug are large and have difficulty getting through the network of tiny vessels that connect the fetal and maternal circulation in the placenta, only small traces of the drug will make their way to the fetus.

Until recently the only way to find out how much of a drug passed through the placental barrier was to draw blood samples immediately after birth from an infant whose mother had been given medication. These studies, however, yielded only limited information. First, since most of the babies examined were born at or near term—i.e., after thirty-eight weeks of gestation—we could learn from blood samples only how much of a drug worked its way across a mature placenta. We could only guess from these studies how much of the substance might have crossed the placenta if it had been given during the early weeks of pregnancy.

Nor could these blood studies on newborn infants tell us anything about how the fetus-child's metabolic system tolerated the drugs. For example, many drugs are metabolized—i.e., broken down and excreted—by the liver

28

and/or the kidney. We know, because we can study the process by examining successive blood samples, how great a dose of a drug an adult liver or kidney can metabolize. But we don't know how great a dose of a drug the immature liver or kidney of a fetus can metabolize.

This sort of information could be extremely valuable. Suppose, for example, that a woman developed a severe bladder infection from a bacteria that was best treated with a powerful antibiotic. And suppose that antibiotic occasionally caused liver damage, so that, when treating the woman, it was necessary to do daily tests to be certain the antibiotic was not damaging the liver. Cases like this are relatively frequent.

Now, suppose that the woman with the severe infection is three months pregnant. You want to use the antibiotic to treat her, but you are afraid to do so because you don't know how much of the antibiotic will pass through the placenta. Nor do you know whether the immature liver of the three-month-old fetus will be able to metabolize the antibiotic. So you have either to substitute a less effective antibiotic, gambling that it will cure the woman, or give the powerful antibiotic you know will be effective and take a chance on damaging the fetus' liver. The doctor is, in effect, put in a position where he must choose between gambling with a woman's life or with the life of her unborn child. It is an extremely uncomfortable and dangerous situation for the doctor, the mother and the child.

Suddenly, with the liberalization of the abortion laws, doctors in Massachusetts were in a position where they could obtain much of the valuable information they needed if they were going to treat pregnant women in a fashion that was safe not only for the mother but for her unborn child. Since the fetuses of the women who were coming to Boston City Hospital for abortions were going to die anyway, why not give the pregnant woman, before her abortion, a medication that might be used to treat other pregnant women? Then, after the fetus had been aborted, its blood and organs could be examined to

29

ber 18, 1973, and I saw to it that it was well advertised. I ran ads in all the Boston papers, I sent letters to Right-to-Life people I knew would be interested in having their say, and I even had copies of the notice hand-delivered to all the doctors at Boston City who might be in any way involved in what was going on. I didn't want them to come back to me later saying that they hadn't had a chance to defend themselves because they didn't know a meeting was being held.''

The meeting was held at the city council chambers in city hall. It started at 10:30 in the morning and lasted till 3:53 in the afternoon. There were several hundred people in attendance. With the exception of the media representatives, most were strong antiabortionists. None of the doctors to whom notices had been hand-delivered were in attendance. (Later, these doctors denied they had ever received any hand-delivered notices.) Councilor O'Neil furnished me with a copy of the transcript, which is 253 pages long.

The flavor of the meeting can best be conveyed by quoting from representative portions of the statements and dialogue taken directly from the transcript. We'll begin with Dapper O'Neil's opening remarks.

Chairman O'Neil: Good morning. First of all I want to welcome you to the hearing this morning. My name is Councillor Albert O'Neil, and on my right is Councillor Lawrence DiCara, and on my left is Councillor Frederick C. Langone, and on my far left Councillor John Kerrigan.

Back on July 30, 1973, I received a letter from Representative Raymond Flynn which I would like to read now for the people who are here.

''Dear Councillor O'Neil:

''It has been brought to my attention that certain inhumane procedures are being practiced at Boston City Hospital and other city medical institutions, both public and

private, following the Supreme Court decision permitting abortions on demand.

"I refer to the *New England Journal of Medicine*, Doctors Philipson, Sabath, and Charles at Boston City Hospital, June 7, 1973, which cites the results of some practices at our own Boston City Hospital.

"I share your views and the views of all right-thinking people that abortions should not be permitted under any circumstances despite the decision of the United States Supreme Court.

"I know you are supporting our efforts to pass a constitutional amendment prohibiting abortions and striking down the high court's ruling. However, the decision has created a situation where there are no regulations on abortion procedures and practices of physicians and hospital administrators.

"I am requesting the filing of an order to require the Committee on Health and Hospitals to conduct an investigation and to hold public hearings with a view toward drafting suitable legislation for the City of Boston and model legislation for the entire Commonwealth.

"Sincerely yours, Raymond L. Flynn."

And then, when I received this on July 30th, I filed on July 30th an order in the Council. This is Docket No. 1828:

"Whereas the recent abhorrent Supreme Court decision on abortion has given rise to some inhumane practices in some of the hospitals and institutions of Boston requiring regulations for the protection of innocent unborn life, therefore be it

"Ordered: That the Committee on Public Health and Hospitals conduct an investigation and hold a public hearing with a view toward drafting suitable legislation for the City of Boston and model legislation for the entire Commonwealth."

33

William A. Nolen, M.D.

Notice of this hearing was advertised in the Boston papers. I have the copies of the advertisement here. . . .

The first advertisement that was in the Boston papers and the notification that was in the local papers was for the consumption of the public, and some of the public have come here today to testify, and I will instruct the staff aides here to circulate amongst those whom I did not call, and if you want to testify, this is still America.

The next speaker was Monsignor Paul Harrington, who represented his Eminence Cardinal Medeiros. Here are representative extracts from his speech. In the first pages he discusses abortion in general; then he moves on to fetal experimentation.

Monsignor Harrington: Truly, whatever may have been its problems, Boston City Hospital has always enjoyed a great reputation and has made medical history for decades—simply by reason of dedicated medical practitioners who were committed to the great ideal and goal of caring for the ills of people, of preventing disease, of curing sickness and of sustaining life. Theirs was a profession of positive and constructive contribution to a large community. Theirs was a program of assisting God and not of trying to replace God. These were men of high ideals, deep commitment, continuing dedication, simple faith and sincere humility. They lived and died— trying to ease pain, to make suffering people more comfortable, to seek cures, to strengthen health, to extend life. These were the interests and the treasures of committed doctors. These giants of the medical world were not concerned with solving the personal, social, economic and political problems of their day; these concerns were never meant to be part of the practice of medicine.

34

The men who made Boston City Hospital great respected and revered life, cared for life, nurtured and sustained life, maintained and extended life—they never extinguished, destroyed or exterminated life.

For decades, therapeutic abortions were never performed at Boston City Hospital; therapeutic abortions were not allowed to be performed because of hospital policy. Yet, in these years, even without modern techniques and therapies and even though the most serious complications of pregnancy found their way to Boston City Hospital—no abortions were performed—the complications were treated—the babies were born and the Boston City Hospital had the lowest maternal mortality rate in the Commonwealth of Massachusetts—and the maternal mortality rate of Boston City Hospital compared most favorably with other hospitals throughout the United States—even with those doing therapeutic abortions.

At least since 1952, we have known that abortions need never be performed because of complications of pregnancy. Doctors Heffernan and Lynch, both renowned obstetricians in the Boston area, after consulting the medical literature in many languages and after considering the complications for which therapeutic abortions were usually performed—renal disease, cardiac complications, hypertension, diabetes, tuberculosis, cardiovascular and pulmonary problems, et cetera—declared that any doctor who performed abortions for any complications of pregnancy did so because he either did not know how to treat the complication or he was too lazy to make the effort—both indictments of the doctor's competency to practice medicine.

Since abortions need not be performed for medical reasons—which is the proper sphere of the medical prac-

35

titioner—doctors are now doing abortions to solve personal, social, economic, and political problems, which is not the sphere of the committed and dedicated doctor.

Abortion is the intentional and deliberate destruction of innocent, helpless, defenseless, voiceless, unborn human life. The unborn baby can do nothing for himself; he depends upon the mercy of his mother and the compassion of her physician—just to be born. It is this tiny, helpless and defenseless baby that the great doctors of the Boston City Hospital in years past were proud and privileged to assist and to deliver.

Now, there is a dangerous, destructive, violent and exterminative element that is creeping into the practice of medicine by some doctors. There are some doctors who, for a fee, are willing to destroy and kill helpless babies because they may not be wanted or may not be loved by their mothers but who would be wanted and loved by thousands of couples who are not blessed by children of their own; because the baby might possibly be born handicapped and impaired and the wishes of such a baby are never consulted and only the feelings of the mother are respected; because the baby, if born, might be poor but abortion has never made poor people rich or removed poor people from welfare rolls; because the baby, if born, might pollute the atmosphere but his parents have two cars in the driveway; because the baby might increase the population and this at a time when we have the lowest birth rate in the history of Boston and the United States; because the baby, if born, would provide inconvenience to his mother, who is more concerned about personal matters.

In the attitudes of some, a questionable value is placed on human life. A baby can only be born if he is wanted and loved, if he is healthy, if he will not be born into poverty, if he will not add to population growth, if he will not

increase pollution, if he is not inconvenient! In all other circumstances, he does not have a right to be born—he is to be aborted—destroyed, killed, extinguished and exterminated—the [sic] fiat of his mother and assisted by her physician, who swore allegiance to an oath that he would care for life, maintain, nurture and sustain life and never destroy life.

It is dangerous to the common good and to the public welfare when individuals assume control and authority over the very lives of others—a right and an authority which they do not have—because authority over human life belongs to God alone—and when these individuals begin to assign a value to human life—when, in fact, every human life has a transcendental value. . . .

Monsignor Harrington then compared, at length, the insidious acceptance of abortion as a "solution" to problems with the Nazi "solution" to the Jewish "problem." Here is the final paragraph in that analogy:

There was a widespread release of destructive drives and destructive activity under the Nazi regime and this was caused by the combined effects of indoctrination with anti-spirituality that resulted in a shift of moral values away from the religious, spiritual and humane; indoctrination with anti-rationalism which resulted in the discrediting and abandonment of reason as the main instrument for decision-making among individuals; a seduction which resulted in pleasurable release of repressed instinctual drives without feelings of guilt. . . .

Finally, Monsignor Harrington returned to the subject of abortion and of fetal experimentation in particular.

If the Boston City Hospital embarks on a pro-abortion

policy, there will result, however silent and subtle, a conspiracy between the Boston City Hospital, its administration, its medical and surgical staffs and expectant mothers to seize control and authority over the lives of unborn babies, then a conspiracy to declare that some unborn babies, if allowed to be born, would have no value, and finally, by violent and destructive methods, the lives of the unborn babies would be snuffed out, destroyed, extinguished, annihilated and exterminated.

We cannot allow the Boston City Hospital and its staff to succumb to the pressures posited by some expectant mothers and certain social reformers and, thereby, turn their back on the hallowed history and tradition of this great municipal institution and violate the sacrosanct ideals, goals and objectives of medicine and good hospital care. . . .

In summary, we object to research and experimentation on live human aborted babies because:

1) The delivery was accomplished by violence;

2) They are human beings with rights and dignity which are not being respected; they are being treated as experimental animals and their humanity is denigrated;

3) They are not informed of the nature of the experiment or its dangers and they are given no opportunity to refuse consent;

4) The concern is for the experimentation and not for the survival of the aborted babies;

5) Such experimentation is immoral, totally objectionable and an unspeakable crime, and neither science nor morality is well served by laboratory experimentation on human beings;

6) Experimentation must first be carried out on animals;

7) The philosophy of "What is useful is good" and the "end justifies the means," which is at the foundation of

experimentation on live human aborted babies, is totally to be rejected.

Because of this presentation and these conclusions, I respectfully urge that such research and experimentation on live human babies be prohibited and interdicted at Boston City Hospital.

Mr. Chairman and members of the Committee, thank you for your courtesy.

Monsignor Harrington's testimony was followed by questions and comments from council members—all of whom warmly praised the monsignor. The next person to testify was Sister Sheila, the administrator of the Laboure Center in South Boston, a Catholic center that provides a wide variety of services for the area's poor. Her testimony reinforced that of Monsignor Harrington. Her final words were these:

Sister Sheila: We support Monsignor Harrington's admiration for the medical research that has gone on at the City Hospital in the hope that this will include the medical care of the people in our area.

However, the frightening prospect that this life may be used for experimental purposes, contrary to the dedication of the medical profession, is rather frightening. It's rather encouraging that in Denver, with the birth of sextuplets recently, over thirty or forty doctors and nurses were on hand to preserve the life of these tiny babies which were born seven weeks prematurely.

With this philosophy of the medical profession we feel that there is great hope for life in all sectors of our country, of our United States, as Mr. O'Neil said.

I will leave to those who are more educated and better prepared than I to support the statement that Monsignor Harrington made.

I would like to leave with each of the Councilmen one

39

William A. Nolen, M.D.

thoughtful picture. It's a question that I would like to put to the doctors of City Hospital, our Councilmen of Boston, and any thoughtful citizen who is really concerned about life and death.

It's the question: Are we for life, or are we for death? And this life is at the beginning of life, at the very beginning.

Our value of life before birth will influence our value of life after birth at all levels of human development and in all phases of family life.

With this, I would like you to study the development of the embryo, the development of the fetus, and ask whether we truly can take God's prerogative of cutting off life at any point.

Thank you for this opportunity.

State Representative Raymond Flynn from South Boston testified next, again along general antiabortion lines. However, the last part of his testimony, an exchange with Councilor O'Neil, is particularly pertinent because of its reference to the district attorney's office:

Chairman O'Neil: Representative, just one question. In the second paragraph of your letter to me which started: "I refer to the *New England Journal of Medicine*, Doctors Philipson, Sabath, and Charles of Boston City Hospital, June 7, 1973, which cites the results of some practices at our own Boston City Hospital."

So there is admission here that these men are performing experiments, and so forth?

Mr. Flynn: In my judgment—and I would like to defer to Dr. Jefferson, who would have more detailed information on that.

However, I do, in fact, know that they have absolutely no legal right.

40

The Constitution of the United States, the Supreme Court decision of January, does not allow this type of conduct to exist, and I think that they are working completely beyond the law, and I think that again I would suggest that perhaps the minutes of this public hearing which the Council was so gracious to have should be made available to the District Attorney for his consideration.

Chairman O'Neil: You can rest assured of that.

Following a friendly exchange between various councilors and Representative Flynn, a Ms. Turner testified. Since she was the only person to say anything in favor of abortion—while still opposing fetal experimentation—some extracts from her speech seem pertinent.

Ms. Turner: I have a variety of identifications.

I am a mother. I happen to be Vice-President of the Area Board, Boston University Medical Center.

I am on the Board of Directors of the Fort Hill Mental Association. I am on the Advisory Board for Boston City Hospital Infant Development Unit.

I am a member of the National Organization of Women. I am a former anti-abortionist, and today I am here as a nurse-mother-taxpayer and Director of COPE. That is C-O-P-E for Coping with the Overall Pregnancy Experience.

It's an organization that I founded and I am presently the Director. I serve pregnant, post-partum, and post-abortion women, and I believe it's the only organization that is serving this mixed bag, as it were, of pregnant women as well as women who have their babies as well as women who have given up their babies. . . .

I think I probably know as well as, if not more than any-

41

one, the seriousness of the question that is being brought up today.

I worked at Boston City Hospital as well as bringing patients there.

I feel very strongly that abortion has to be available at City Hospital. I cannot support the experimentation, though.

I am dealing with, as I said, women, couples, and fathers who meet at COPE to talk about their feelings during pregnancy and post-partum as well as having a weekly group of women coming in to talk about their feelings about having had an abortion.

My commitment is to take people where they are at and not turn anybody away. This is why we started the post-abortion group.

I also started the post-abortion group to improve the quality of life, to help women work through their feelings. It is a serious situation, so that they will not get pregnant again, not have another unborn pregnancy.

The rate of repeat abortions is quite high, and I am committed to preventing another abortion happening, another unwanted pregnancy.

Research has come out at Beth Israel Hospital, a research team of three females, psychiatrists, that followed women who have gone through an abortion for a year and a half, the 70 percent of women who have an abortion that are not on any kind of birth control.

There are unconscious reasons that women get pregnant. We talked about the innocence of the fetus. I am also here to maintain that there is an innocence in mothers. There are reasons that people get pregnant besides failed birth control.

There is no form of birth control that is adequate. I got pregnant on the IUD, which is supposed to be 99 percent

sure, and also got pregnant on the coil. One pregnancy I kept, and the other pregnancy I terminated.

So there is the innocence of the fetus, yes. You talked about people being born as equals. Well, who is more equal? The unborn fetus or the mature individual that has made it through twenty years of life and is faced with a pregnancy that they haven't planned for and feel will disrupt and in some cases ruin their lives? . . .

There is a high incidence of juvenile delinquency for the babies that were not planned and not wanted. There is a high incidence of child abuse that kids get. On the argument of putting it up for adoption, there are single women and married women who don't want their babies and, with all of their morning sickness, are keeping their pregnancy, and we are supporting them through their pregnancy, much like the people from Birthright. People want to keep their pregnancies. We are there, too.

Chairman O'Neil: We will make a television star out of your baby. He photographs well.

Ms. Turner: I have lost my train of thought, however.

The women who come and want to keep their babies, we are supporting them, too, so that I am probably a different speaker than you have had before.

I am not an anti-abortionist, and I am not a pro-abortionist, except that I believe in the right of choice, and that is what I want to come down and say.

Oh, I know what I was going to say. I am concerned about adoptions. The pat answer is "All right, we will support you through this pregnancy, even though it's not wanted, and help you make a decision of whether or not to give this baby up for adoption."

The popular scene at this point is for people to keep their babies.

For the women who, for their own moral reasons, are

keeping their pregnancies, adoption isn't the pat answer.

The adoption agencies realize that more and more women are keeping the pregnancies that they haven't planned, so I am concerned about the support of preventing higher rates of juvenile delinquency and higher rates of child abuse for the women who are not giving the baby up for adoption and are keeping it.

So that it's not a simple solution. It's not the unborn fetus or the mother. It's both that have to be taken into consideration.

I am certainly going to push for City Hospital having an abortion clinic for those people who ask for it, and for those people who don't opt for it, there are groups to support them through their pregnancies.

So that I am concerned about the right of choice being made available.

Finally, the council committee heard the testimony of prominent members of the Right to Life organization. Here are excerpts:

Chairman O'Neil: May I have the Representatives of the Massachusetts Citizens for Life of 430 Center Street in Newton? Dr. Jefferson?

May I have your name and address and your title, please?

Dr. Jefferson: Yes. I am Dr. Mildred F. Jefferson, Assistant Clinical Professor of Surgery at Boston University School of Medicine and Vice-President and member of the Board of Directors, Massachusetts Citizens for Life.

Chairman O'Neil: And the gentleman on your right?

Dr. Stanton: My name is Joseph R. Stanton. I am a practicing physician in Boston. I am a member of the Massachusetts Citizens for Life.

Chairman O'Neil: The gentleman on your left?

44

Mr. Smith: I am Professor James W. Smith of Boston College Law School. . . .

Chairman O'Neil: Thank you very much. You may proceed, my dear lady.

Dr. Jefferson: Thank you.

Honorable gentlemen of the Council, I am honored to be here today but somewhat sad because on any medical tradition based on the Hippocratic oath which requires from the doctor a standard of purity and holiness we would not have occasion of having this kind of hearing.

I will not leave a prepared statement of my testimony because Dr. Stanton, who will present most of the medical testimony, has one which will give you the facts.

We have printed materials which should be the knowledge of every person who is concerned about ending the life that is beginning.

I am sorry I must take a few extra minutes because some issues have been introduced which have served simply to confuse the issues here.

We did not have a week to discuss all of the difficult problems involved in abortion and who has them and why. We have been honored with this time to help call attention to what perhaps is one of the most flagrant abuses not only of the unborn child but perhaps of the women who may not have known what they were agreeing to or consenting to when they said, "We will participate in your experiment.". . .

So, indeed, if you look into the matter of the woman who is allowing or agreeing to an experiment—and Dr. Stanton will discuss the one that Representative Flynn called attention to—we see in that that the ages given for the women who participated in that experiment were as young as fifteen years.

We cannot help asking the question: How at age fifteen could one really give informed consent?

45

William A. Nolen, M.D.

Whoever signed that permission, we would like to know: How could they give truly informed consent if they were not aware of the increased risks and complications in the very young teen-agers who have been subjected to abortion? How could anyone counselling them inform them enough for them to have informed consent if they were not familiar with the work of Dr. Carol Cole in Canada who called attention to that in her observation of teen-agers between fourteen and eighteen, that one-third of them were sterile after their abortion experience?

After Dr. Jefferson had finished, Dr. Stanton asked for and was given permission to read a statement which he said would take thirteen minutes to read. His statement was supportive of Dr. Jefferson's, but he made two additional points: (1) He implied that some of the fetuses reported on in the *New England Journal of Medicine* article must have been alive at the time of the study; unless their hearts were beating it would have been impossible to get useful blood samples from them. (2) He mentioned that, despite the great increase in the number of abortions being performed in New York State since the liberalization of abortion laws in 1971, the incidence of child abuse "was skyrocketing."

(At the risk of emphasizing the obvious, I might mention here that at Dapper's hearing no attempt was made to restrict testimony to the issue supposedly under consideration, i.e., fetal experimentation. This was a public hearing and Dapper, as chairman, was able to allow anyone to ramble on about any subject he deemed even remotely a part of the problem.)

After the testimony of Doctors Jefferson and Stanton and that of Professor James W. Smith of Boston College Law School—who proposed an antifetal experimentation bill—the following exchange between Councilor O'Neil and Councilor

46

Tierney occurred. I quote it only because it gives some of the flavor of the meeting:

Councillor Tierney: No, no. Dr. Stanton started to make a statement about what some person told him, and that, of course, is hearsay, but this isn't a court of law, and I ask that the recorder would hold it off the record and not put it on the record to help give us some direction.

We are a public forum, and let's find out what this situation is. I would ask that the Chair would rule on that.

Chairman O'Neil: Overruled.

Councillor Piemonte: Mr. Chairman, I move that any statement made which is hearsay be made in executive session.

Chairman O'Neil: I rule that any statement to be made here, as the Chairman, will be made in public.

Councillor Piemonte: I appeal the ruling of the Chair.

Chairman O'Neil: Objection overruled.

Councillor Piemonte: Take a vote on it. When the Chair overrules, we will take a vote.

Councillor Tierney: No.

Chairman O'Neil: I have always advocated that when people are paying taxes in this city and we have public hearings, there will be nothing in the back room or anything else. That is my attitude, Councillor Tierney. (Applause)

Councillor Piemonte: Mr. Chairman, I appeal the ruling of the Chair, because if somebody came in and said that that women in the yellow and gold coat in the third row is neglecting her children, it shouldn't be made public, because there is no truth to it.

First of all, there is no such woman in the third row. Now, use your bean.

47

William A. Nolen, M.D.

Chairman O'Neil: You bet your life I will use my bean.
Councillor Piemonte: Don't play to the audience.
Chairman O'Neil: I will show you how to use the bean.
Is Dr. Gottlieb here?
Dr. David Charles here?
Dr. Samson Amusa here?
Dr. Jose Aubert?
Dr. Lester Benn?
Dr. Matthew Burrell?
Dr. Hee Man Chie?
Dr. Bruce Davidson?
Dr. Joseph Egharevba?
Dr. Lidia Frete?
Dr. Enrique Giminez-Jimeno?
Dr. Kenneth Hekman?
Dr. Wilfredo Linares?
Dr. Farid Louis?
Dr. Ramon Miro?
Dr. Samuel Nun?
Dr. Efrain Perez-Pena?
Dr. Felix Sassano?
Dr. Paul Toselli?
Are any of them here?

These gentlemen were not notified by mail; it was hand-delivered to them. And it's quite obvious to me that none of them showed up here, so somebody is hiding something here.

After the antiabortion, antiexperiment group testified, a few of those in attendance were given the opportunity to defend the policies at Boston City Hospital. Herbert Gleason, corporation counsel of the city and acting chairman of the Board of Health and Hospitals, presented their case fairly thoroughly.

* * *

Mr. Gleason: I don't have a prepared statement, Councillor, but just let me respond to some of the things that have been said during this long morning and into the afternoon, not only in a contentious way, because it's a problem that very much concerns all of us.

It concerns me both as a lawyer and as an official of the Department, and it concerns Mr. Guiney as an official of the hospital and in the proper regulations involved in the medical field.

I want to emphasize as strongly as I possibly can that we have absolutely no knowledge whatsoever of any illegal activity in connection with this or any other experimental undertaking or any undertaking whatsoever at the Boston City Hospital, and if our information is insufficient, if we should know about something, I hope it will be brought to our attention promptly, because there is no need to wait until your honorable body or the legislature or the Governor or the Congress or anybody else tells us not to do illegal things, for us to stop doing illegal things, if they are going on.

But, as I say again, we have no knowledge of it, and that means that these patients were aborted for therapeutic reasons.

Now, if that is not so, we would like to know it, but it's represented in the whole description of the study, and the article about it.

It's represented by Dr. Charles to us that the patients involved here had already made the determination to have a therapeutic abortion before anything was done. So that let's be clear about that. If our information on that is not correct, we want to be told. But that is our understanding, and it was on that basis that the study was approved.

Secondly, to our knowledge, no experiment was done on a living fetus. I don't like that expression, and I know

49

William A. Nolen, M.D.

that professionally it tangles up a lot of the facts and is not really an accurate description, but it's been used here this morning.

None of the fetal material was alive when it was tested in the pathology laboratory, which those of you who are familiar with the Boston City Hospital know is geographically far separated from the ob-gyn building. So that the fetuses, in any event, had to be transported from the ob-gyn operating room across Albany Street to the pathology lab, and by definition a fetus within a time span of this amount, let us say, can no longer survive outside its mother's womb.

So I think it can be fairly confidently assumed that what has been alleged here this morning and what has been implied here this morning would certainly lead us to make an even closer analysis than we have already made of that question, but it's our understanding and it's been represented to us that there was no experimentation on living fetal material, and none would be permitted, and none is permitted by the Boston City Hospital.

So, if it's going on, it shouldn't go on, and we again don't need legislation to stop that because we don't believe in it.

Following Mr. Gleason's testimony was some rather devastating testimony from Rosetta Harrington which, the record shows, Mr. O'Neil was anxious to get to the media.

Chairman O'Neil: Just one second, please. Is Miss Harrington here, the nurse from BCH?

Mr. Gleason: Yes, she is.

Chairman O'Neil: Mr. Guiney, would you yield your chair for just a moment? I will ask the press to listen to this lady.

50

Miss Harrington, will you identify yourself and make a statement, please?

Ms. Harrington: My name is Rosetta Harrington. I worked for the Boston City Hospital from October, 1963, to November, 1971, and one of the main reasons that I left was because of all the abortions they were doing at that time. This was before the law was passed.

They were doing many saline abortions, most of them being done during the daytime, and you know, they would go down to the wards to labor, and they would come back to us. I would be on the delivery floor, and we would take care of the mothers.

This is not what I rejected, taking care of the mothers. They wanted to do these abortions at night, also, and I said flatly No, I would not be part of it.

At the time there were five registered nurses working at night on the delivery floor. Three of them said No, and two said that they would, and the doctors told us flatly if we did not go ahead with this, they would have our jobs.

So I went to my own lawyer, and he said they had no right to take my job, that I had every right to say No to this procedure, and we went to the front office and told them, and they presented it to the Board of Trustees, from what I hear, and it was okayed after this.

But we were really afraid of losing our jobs over this.

I have taken live aborted babies to the nurseries during this time and have gotten a lot of harassment from those people down there: "Why are you bringing us these specimens, because now we have to do them up, to get rid of them?"

Chairman O'Neil: You what, Ma'am?

Ms. Harrington: This is what they say you know. They said to us, "Why are you bringing these specimens, be-

51

CARNEGIE LIBRARY
LIVINGSTONE COLLEGE
SALISBURY, N. C. 28144

cause I am just going to leave it in the corner until it dies.''

I am very nervous.

Chairman O'Neil: Please don't be nervous. I am very interested in what you are saying.

Ms. Harrington: This is one of the reasons why I left. They were doing them at the time, and I can't give you months, but I can give you: I left in November of 1971, and they were being done that year, so this is about all I have to say. I think that is enough.

Her testimony was contradicted rather strongly by Mrs. Hargraves, a representative of the Boston City Hospital nurses:

Chairman O'Neil: Mrs. Hargraves, do you have a statement you would like to make?

Mrs. Hargraves: Yes, very much.

Chairman O'Neil: Proceed.

Mrs. Hargraves: I would like to speak on two accounts.

I feel strongly that I want to make it quite clear that I have no question in my mind about the courage of Boston City Hospital nurses or the courage of Boston City Hospital nurses in 1963 or 1971.

The Boston City Hospital nurses initiated the development of a position statement which not only is a position statement of nurses in the State of Massachusetts at the present time but is widely circulated throughout the country, and more recently medicine is accepting the same statement, that people have the right to their own beliefs, and nurses and doctors cannot be forced to participate in abortions if they make it clear and are very forthright in saying so. They do not have to participate.

This is so at the present time at Boston City Hospital.

It is our position throughout the State of Massachusetts, and I feel very hopeful about it, but then we hope that people will search their hearts and minds and become very clear in their own minds whether they feel they will or they will not participate.

It is the law of the land that women have the right to abortion at the present time. Right or wrong, it is the law.

It is the policy of the City of Boston that they will abide in the Department of Health and Hospitals by the law of the land.

It is the policy of the Department of Nursing, with strong support from the administration and the Board, that no nurse in the Department of Health and Hospitals against her will will be forced to participate in the care of patients who are undergoing abortion.

We do not have abortion for the purpose of experimentation under any circumstances that I know.

We do not in any way participate in experimentation on live fetuses that I know.

I know of no situation whereby a nurse is being forced to participate at the present time. If there is any such evidence, I would be glad to have it, and I would be glad to follow through on it.

I would like nurses to come to work at the Boston City Hospital in our Out Patient Department, and I feel that they will find this kind of fair play.

Chairman O'Neil: Mrs. Hargraves, as the Chairman of this Committee, when I receive communications from people, whether it be right or whether it be wrong, and it's signed, it is my sworn duty to look into all aspects, and I will dedicate myself now to a lot of time at the City Hospital.

If there is any evidence that I can dig up, I will inform you, Mr. Gleason, of it, and we have the finest hospital in the world down there, in my opinion. The nurses are tre-

53

William A. Nolen, M.D.

mendous people, but if there are any animosities here today because Mrs. Harrington was courageous enough to
state that she wanted no part of it or she'd lose her job
and she also saw abortions of young girls, matured young
girls under age, then it's my duty to look into this, as
Councillor Langone has stated.

If there are delegations, then we will go right from the
very beginning. My hearing will be continued until I put
my investigation together and we bring everybody back.

I think you will agree with me that when I had hand-
delivered nineteen notices to nineteen doctors that were
immediately affected and not one single one of them
showed up here, then I have suspicion in my mind and I
intend to clear that suspicion.

The rest of the testimony was, for the most part, a restate-
ment of all that the first speakers had said. At 3:53 Councilor
O'Neil adjourned the meeting.

5

Dapper was as good as his word. When the hearing ended and transcripts were available, he took them to the district attorney's office. Newman Flanagan, an assistant district attorney, promised the press and the people of Boston that his office would look into what was going on at Boston City Hospital. He was quoted as saying that "while action will be dormant for a little while, there is some merit to the complaints that have been made so far." He was also quoted as saying that "a full investigation and the nature of it may be made public by mid-January."

It is difficult to argue that, at least technically, the physicians who had done the antibiotic study were not guilty of fetal experimentation. According to their report, the fetuses, at the time of abortion, ranged in age from ten to twenty-two weeks. Supposedly the fetuses were being aborted for therapeutic reasons. But even if this were not true, and the mothers were simply exercising their newly acquired constitutional right to have an abortion, as a matter of choice, before the fe-

tus was twenty-four weeks old, according to *Roe* v. *Wade* the abortions would still have been legal. Nowhere in the article is there a statement as to whether or not any of the fetuses were alive when aborted, but it is not unreasonable to assume, as both Dr. Jefferson and Dr. Stanton did, that this was, in fact, the case. Whether the fetuses could have been kept alive for more than a few minutes must remain a matter of conjecture. In all probability, as we will see later, this could not have been accomplished.

The article did claim that the abortions were "therapeutic." Since the terms will be used frequently I had best make it clear that all abortions may be, and generally are, classified as either "elective" or "therapeutic." These labels, to a physician, are, or should be, self-explanatory, but since this may not be true for a lay person, I shall elaborate on them.

An elective abortion is one that is done not because it is necessary to protect the health or life of the pregnant woman, but simply because the woman chooses—elects, if you will—to have it done. She is pregnant, she does not want to have a child, and so she elects to have an abortion. The doctor who performs an elective abortion is destroying the fetus, emptying the uterus, not because by so doing he will protect the health of his patient; he is performing the abortion only because his patient has asked him to do so. Those who fight for abortion on demand are fighting for the right of a woman to have an elective abortion.

A therapeutic abortion, on the other hand, is one that is done to protect the life and/or health of the pregnant woman. Suppose, for example, that a woman with severe heart disease becomes pregnant. The pregnancy will put more strain on her heart than her heart can tolerate. Her doctor feels that it will be dangerous—possibly fatal—for the woman to carry this pregnancy to term. In such a case, if the doctor, with the woman's permission, performs an abortion, that abortion would be classified as therapeutic; the abortion would be a

56

form of therapy for the woman, in that it would protect her heart from whatever extra strain the pregnancy might put on it.

A woman who has diseased kidneys, a woman with severe diabetes, a woman who has just had an operation for breast cancer; in these and other situations a pregnancy might be dangerous or fatal for the mother, and an abortion carried out on such a patient would be classified as therapeutic.

Unfortunately, though in many cases the difference between elective and therapeutic is clear, there is a middle ground where the distinction becomes blurred.

For example, for the woman who becomes wildly psychotic when she discovers she is pregnant, an abortion would probably be classified as therapeutic by most doctors. On the other hand, suppose she becomes transiently depressed when she learns she is pregnant; would an abortion under those circumstances be classified as therapeutic? Probably not, except by those doctors who are willing to abort anyone at any time and like to protect themselves—if such protection is necessary— by categorizing the abortion as "therapeutic." The woman, with or without sedation, will probably come out of her mild depression very quickly. (To use another example: aborting a woman to cure her of a mild depression would be like amputating a leg to cure an ingrown toenail.)

Dr. Joseph Stanton, as we saw, testified that in his opinion it is never necessary to do a therapeutic abortion, that a capable doctor who is willing to work hard can get even the most critically ill patient safely through a pregnancy.

Most doctors, however, would agree that for certain patients with severe diseases, such as those I have offered as examples, an abortion is reasonable treatment. It should be done and would be classified as therapeutic. And few doctors would oppose the right of another doctor to perform a therapeutic abortion, though they themselves might, on religious or other grounds, not be willing to do even those abortions.

William A. Nolen, M.D.

On the other hand, of the approximately 1,115,000 abortions done in the United States, it is doubtful that more than 10,000 could be honestly classified as therapeutic, even by those doctors with the most liberal attitude toward abortion. The vast majority of these abortions are elective, done solely because the woman wants the abortion. There may be social or economic reasons that pro-abortionists deem reasonable as justification for performance of the abortions, but they are not done to protect the life or health of the mother and so cannot be classified as therapeutic.

In the article by Charles et al., the article that precipitated Dapper O'Neil's open hearing and led, eventually, to the Edelin case, the authors stated, as I have said, that the abortions were being done for therapeutic reasons. They did not say, however, what these therapeutic reasons were. Since many of the abortions were done on teen-age girls who would generally be expected to be in good health, I suspect that the label "therapeutic" was rather loosely applied, perhaps to include those pregnant girls suffering from "emotional distress" or even "morning sickness." In the article there is absolutely no evidence that it would have been detrimental to the health of these patients if the pregnancies were allowed to continue. I suspect—and again, till the "grave robbers'" case is resolved we shall probably not have the answer—that most of the abortions done in this study would have been classified as "elective" by the vast majority of physicians.

At the Meeker County Hospital, where I practice, about 300 babies are delivered each year. In the seventeen years that I have been practicing here not a single doctor who practices obstetrics has found it necessary to perform a therapeutic abortion. Nor, they have told me, have any of the doctors on our staff—even those who have been here longer than I— ever found it necessary to refer a patient who needed a therapeutic abortion. Two of the older doctors on the staff, who, combined, have been doing general practice with obstetrics

for seventy years, have told me they have never had to perform a therapeutic abortion or treated a patient who needed
one. Now that amniocentesis is becoming more prevalent so
that it will become possible to diagnose birth defects while the
fetus is still in the uterus, chances are we will occasionally
find a patient who will want a "therapeutic" abortion because
she is carrying a deformed child. But true therapeutic abortions, necessary to save a mother's life, have always been ex-
ceedingly rare and, I suspect, with improved maternal care
will be all but obsolete in the very near future.

This is probably as good a place as any to make one other
fact clear. At the time of the Edelin trial there were many
Bostonians, including reporters, who suggested that the only
reason Edelin was brought to trial was to gain publicity for the
prosecutor, Newman Flanagan. Even the *Harvard Crimson*,
in an editorial on Wednesday, December 15, 1976, had this to
say: "And even given his contention that a child had been
born, Flanagan could not prove that the alleged human life
was vioble [sic] or that Edelin had intentionally harmed it. All
Flanagan could do was argue against making patients and
their doctors 'the absolute judge of what the law is in this
country.' What Flanagan hoped to do with the abortion law
for the sake of his own political mileage was clear."
Presumably, what the *Crimson* was suggesting was that
Newman Flanagan prosecuted Edelin only to gain additional
prominence so that when Garrett Byrne—who is in his seven-
ties and had been the district attorney of Suffolk County for
twenty-one years—finally retired, Attorney Flanagan would
be elected his successor. I can say that if that motivation was
clear to the editorial writer of the *Crimson*, it was not clear to
me. Both Garrett Byrne and Newman Flanagan, in my conversations with them, stated explicitly that they had had absolutely no desire to become entangled in any sort of law-medi-

59

cine battle that would, predictably, be not only distasteful but would be likely to polarize the entire city. I believed them then; I believe them now.

While the press was publicizing Dapper's fetal experimentation hearing and the district attorney's office was trying to decide what action, if any, to take, activity on the obstetrics-gynecology service at Boston City Hospital continued as hectic as ever. In fact, for Dr. Edelin, the work load increased substantially.

As I've already noted, in January of 1973, when the Supreme Court struck down restrictive antiabortion state laws, the obstetrical-gynecological residents at Boston City Hospital were almost overwhelmed with their increased work load. But at least there were six residents on the resident staff who were willing to perform abortions. Unfortunately, when Dr. Edelin became chief resident on July 1, 1973—the traditional date when new interns begin their training and more experienced residents move up the ladder of responsibility—of all the residents in the obstetrical-gynecological house staff only two, one of whom was Dr. Edelin, were willing to perform abortions. This meant that in addition to his new responsibilities as chief resident, Dr. Edelin had to perform approximately three times the number of abortions he had become accustomed to doing. To say that he had a heavy work load would be a gross understatement.

However, he made the necessary adjustments and, apparently, performed his duties very efficiently.

On September 21, 1973, a young woman whom we will call Alice Roe came to the outpatient department at Boston City Hospital. In all matters related to Ms. Roe's personal life I have to rely on verbal reports from doctors, lawyers and nurses, since, by mutual agreement of attorney Newman Flanagan, who prosecuted the Edelin case, and attorney William Homans, who defended Edelin, Ms. Roe's real name was never made known to the press or the public, and she was

not required to testify at Dr. Edelin's trial. Seventeen years old and a student, Alice Roe is, reportedly, of West Indian extraction. She was pregnant, as became evident after her abortion, with a black child. She was there because she wanted an abortion.

The first doctor to see Alice Roe was Dr. Hugh Holtrop, a board-certified obstetrician-gynecologist who happened to be working in the outpatient department on that date.

"It was late in the day, when I saw her," Dr. Holtrop told me when I talked with him in February 1977. "I spent almost an hour with her. The social workers had gone home by then so I did the counseling myself. I'm not going to tell you anything specific about her—that was four years ago, and if she was entitled to privacy then, she is certainly entitled to it now—but I will say this: in my opinion, for that girl, an abortion was literally a matter of life or death. After talking with her and examining her, I felt she was twenty or twenty-one weeks pregnant; but even if I'd agreed with Dr. Giminez, who, as you know, examined her later and decided she was twenty-four weeks pregnant, I'd have gone along with her decision to have an abortion."

Why Alice Roe had waited so long before seeking an abortion is not absolutely clear. The best information I could get—and this came from someone extremely close to her—was that she had waited, hoping that she would abort spontaneously, because she was extremely frightened of her father. He was apparently the dominant figure in the household, and Alice Roe was afraid of what he might do to both her and her boyfriend—again, my information is that the pregnancy was not the result of a casual affair—if he found out she was pregnant. Finally, when it became almost impossible to conceal her condition any longer, she had confided in her mother, who had persuaded her to seek an abortion.

On this first visit, on September 21, Dr. Holtrop agreed to arrange an abortion for Ms. Roe. Dr. Holtrop was then doing

61

6

On the morning of October 1 Dr. Holtrop visited Alice Roe in the hospital. He looked through the admission record and noted that Dr. Giminez had estimated the fetal age at twenty-four weeks. This did not disturb Dr. Holtrop. He, after all, was a board-certified obstetrician-gynecologist with several years of practice experience; Giminez was a relatively inexperienced second-year resident. It is not unusual for two doctors, examining the same patient, to make different estimations of the duration of pregnancy. When that happens, it would be expected that the more experienced doctor's estimation would be the more accurate.

On October 1 the aminoglutethamide study was carried out without difficulty, and on the morning of October 2, when the study was completed, Alice Roe was taken to the room where saline abortions were performed. Before being brought to this room, the nurses, on Dr. Edelin's orders, had emptied Alice's bladder by catheterization and had given her an injection of ten milligrams of Valium, a sedative. In the saline abortion

room she was met by Dr. Edelin; this was the first time he had seen Alice Roe since he had been introduced to her by Dr. Holtrop in the outpatient department on September 21. Dr. Edelin looked over her record and noted the discrepancy between Dr. Holtrop's and Dr. Giminez' estimation of the fetal age. Dr. Edelin then palpated—i.e., pressed on—Alice Roe's abdomen in order to feel the uterus, and he concluded, as had Dr. Holtrop, that she was about twenty-two weeks pregnant.

Dr. Edelin then explained to Ms. Roe what steps he would be following in performing the saline abortion. First, he would inject a local anesthetic into the skin of her abdomen, overlying the uterus. Once the skin and underlying tissues of the abdominal wall were anesthetized, he would pass a longer, hollow needle through the abdominal wall and on in through the muscular wall of the uterus. She would experience no pain as the needle passed through the wall of the uterus since the wall of the uterus is insensitive. Once through the uterine wall, the needle would, hopefully, penetrate the amniotic sac, the sac of fluid in which the fetus floats and moves about while in the uterus. Dr. Edelin would then withdraw a very small amount of amniotic fluid—just enough fluid to make certain that the end of the needle was, indeed, in the amniotic sac—and then he would inject 200 cubic centimeters (about seven ounces) of a concentrated salt solution into the amniotic sac. It was essential that the doctor know with certainty that the end of the needle was in the amniotic sac, because if it were not—if, for example, the concentrated salt solution were injected into the blood stream of the patient—she would almost certainly develop immediate, severe convulsions and die. Assuming the saline solution were injected into the amniotic sac, the woman would ordinarily go into labor within twenty-four hours and the fetus and placenta would be expelled shortly thereafter. In the unlikely event that the fetus were living when expelled, it was the policy at Boston City Hospital to send the fetus to the pediatric intensive care unit.

After finishing his explanation, Dr. Edelin attempted to perform the saline abortion. He was unable to get the needle into the amniotic sac. Each time, despite having introduced the needle its entire length (the standard needle used in saline abortions is 3½ inches long), instead of clear amniotic fluid he got back blood. He decided Alice Roe had an anterior placenta, i.e., a placenta that was attached to the front wall of the uterus. In all probability the needle was entering the placenta after passing through the abdominal and uterine walls, and that was why he could not get the needle into the amniotic sac. After three or four unsuccessful attempts, Dr. Edelin decided to give up for the morning and Ms. Roe was returned to her room.

That afternoon, the afternoon of October 2, 1973, Alice Roe was brought back to the saline abortion room, and Dr. Edelin again tried to perform the abortion. This time he tried inserting the needle at a different angle, hoping to avoid the placenta. Again, after several attempts, he was unsuccessful. He explained to Alice Roe what the difficulties were. He then briefly left the saline abortion room to seek the advice of Dr. James Penza, the associate director of obstetrics. Dr. Penza told Dr. Edelin not to make any further attempts at saline abortion that day. Instead, the next morning, he—Dr. Penza—would attempt to do a saline abortion. If he, too, were unsuccessful, then Dr. Edelin would immediately proceed to do the abortion by hysterotomy. (A hysterotomy is a procedure, sometimes called a mini-Caesarean section, in which the abdomen and then the uterus are opened and the fetus is removed. It is an alternative method of abortion that can be used when saline abortion fails.)

On the morning of October 3 Alice Roe was brought to Operating Room #2 of the gynecology department. Dr. Edelin helped her move from the stretcher onto the operating table. Dr. Penza then attempted to perform a saline abortion but with no more success than Dr. Edelin had had. Dr. Penza then

confirmed the decision they had made the previous day, that Dr. Edelin should now proceed with abortion by hysterotomy. Dr. Edelin told the operating room nurses to prepare for surgery—lay out the instruments and drapes and wash the patient's abdomen with an antiseptic solution. Then Dr. Edelin went out into the corridor where he found Steve Teich, a third-year medical student from Boston University, who agreed to assist him. They scrubbed up and, with Alice Roe "asleep" under a general anesthetic, Dr. Edelin proceeded to perform the hysterotomy, which we will discuss in much greater detail later. When the fetus was removed, the nurse placed it in a paper box and transferred it to the pathology department at Boston City Hospital. There it was examined by Dr. Frank Juliano Fallico, a resident pathologist, who put the fetus in a two-quart plastic container that contained the 10 percent formalin solution commonly used to preserve, i.e., prevent decay of, human tissue. He screwed a plastic top on the container and set it aside in the surgical pathology cutting room. (At Boston City Hospital the rule for residents in pathology was that if a fetus twenty weeks or over were sent to the pathology department, they were not to dissect it but were to notify their superiors in the department. Since this fetus had been labeled "twenty-two weeks" by Dr. Edelin, this was the policy Dr. Fallico followed.)

On or about October 5 the fetus, in its container, was transferred to the morgue, where it remained till early December of 1973.

7

As a result of the publicity generated by Dapper O'Neil's hearings, the district attorney's office was under pressure to look into activities at Boston City Hospital, particularly into policies in the ob-gyn department. As Assistant District Attorney Newman Flanagan told me during one of our many conversations, "We were getting phone calls from a lot of people—nurses, right-to-lifers, doctors and just plain citizens of Boston who had been stirred up by Dapper's hearings and the coverage in the press. We had to do something."

"What was this 'grave-robber' law that the researchers were supposed to have broken?" I asked.

"That was just a name for a law that was on the books that was necessary in the old days when medical schools needed bodies to dissect and there were people who would dig up freshly buried cadavers and sell them to the medical school. The law really had very little to do with this experimentation business, but the press liked the label so they used it."

William A. Nolen, M.D.

"It does have an interesting ring to it," I said. "But if that wasn't the law that applied, what law did?"

"Really it was a matter of unlawful use of a body," Newman said. "The case is still pending [this conversation took place on May 13, 1977] but generally it's our contention that the doctors who did the experimentation didn't have proper, informed authorization to do what they did to those fetuses,* particularly if they were alive when aborted, as some of the testimony suggests.

"But, as you know—since the experimentation case is still pending—Dapper's hearings just got the pot boiling. Indirectly, he led us to the Edelin case. What happened was that late in November and early in December of 1973, after he had stirred things up, our office began to get a lot of calls from people who claimed that there were two big babies in bottles down at the Boston City Morgue. It was even brought up on one of the local television or radio phone-in shows—I can't remember for sure which one. Some of the callers—nurses or aides or janitors at the hospital—claimed actually to have seen these babies. Others had just heard about them. You can imagine how fast a story like that travels around a Catholic city like Boston. Anyway, we had no alternative but to look into the matter and either confirm it or make a statement that said it was nonsense. So I called Curtis—George Curtis, the Suffolk County coroner—and asked him to visit the morgue and see what, if anything, was there. Sure enough, he found two babies in jars. Massachusetts law says that any baby over twenty weeks that's born live and dies has to have both a birth and death certificate. If the baby's over twenty weeks and it's born dead, it still needs a death certificate. Curtis took one look at these two and knew they were over twenty weeks. Since they didn't have any certificates—birth or death—he

*See Dr. Mildred Jefferson's statement at Dapper's open hearing.

70

took possession of them. Then he called me and told me what he'd found and done.

"Now we were well into December of '73. Garrett and I talked it over. As he told you, he didn't think our office should get involved in any abortion case if we could help it. Garrett's been DA a long time—Dever [Governor Paul Dever] appointed him in 1952 when the incumbent DA died. Garrett was elected at the next election in 1954 and he's been reelected every four years since then. He knows the law, he knows Massachusetts politics, and he knows what we can do and what we can't do. He knew, as he told you, that an abortion case might be dynamite, and he wasn't going to get involved in one if it didn't seem proper. On the other hand, right is right and if some of the things that were going on at Boston City were illegal, then we had an obligation to take action. We decided to get more information and see if there were a case in this."

"So what did you do next?" I said. I'd read copies of so many legal decisions and transcripts of hearings that I knew most of the facts fairly well, but the time sequences kept getting jumbled.

"I asked Dr. Curtis to do autopsies on the babies," Newman said. "We were most interested in the Roe baby since that was the biggest one and had been delivered by hysterotomy. I wondered if possibly that baby had been alive at the time it was taken from the mother and, if so, if there was some way that Dr. Curtis could tell that. If it were alive when it was removed from the mother, then we had a whole different ball game. Now instead of just an abortion case, we'd be dealing with a case of murder or at least manslaughter. If that were the situation, then there was only one honest thing to do—prosecute the person who had committed the crime."

So in December, on the order of Newman Flanagan, Dr. Curtis performed an autopsy on "Baby Boy Roe." When he received the autopsy report and after consultation with Gar-

71

rett Byrne, Newman Flanagan decided to convene the grand jury. He felt that there was sufficient evidence to indict Dr. Kenneth Edelin for manslaughter; now he had to persuade the grand jury that this was indeed the case.

8

Newman Flanagan is, by common consent of all the lawyers I spoke to, not only an excellent lawyer but a very persuasive, eloquent man. He is about 5'10", has a slight paunch, is almost bald and has a round, friendly, obviously Irish face. He has a taste for flamboyant, colorful neckties—not the sort of neckwear one would find on the Yankee lawyers he often opposes in the courtroom. I watched him in action in April, 1976, when the Edelin case was appealed to the Massachusetts Supreme Court, and again in December, while waiting to ask him some more questions about the Edelin case. On that occasion I sat in the back of the courtroom while he summed up his case against a man accused of murdering a storekeeper in an attempted robbery. He speaks fluently, forcefully, obviously prepares his cases very well, and it was easy for me to believe that if anyone would be able to convince a jury that his cause was just, Newman Flanagan was that man. (It is well to remember that juries are composed of ordinary men and women. Lawyers and doctors are automatically excused from jury

duty, and the very rich and powerful usually find excuses for not serving. The lawyer who looks like he is one of the "regular" people is wise. A "rumpled" look is almost a trademark for some lawyers—cultivated, the way William Buckley cultivates his tousled hair and askew but conservative tie. Newman Flanagan is not rumpled, but, I suspect, he is aware that his exotic ties help him acquire a certain rapport with—possibly even sympathy from—a jury.)

Those who are summoned to testify before a grand jury are not allowed to bring their lawyer, if they have retained one, with them. The witness may, of course, get advice from his or her lawyer before appearing and, after testifying, may discuss his testimony with his lawyer. A witness is not supposed to discuss his testimony with anyone other than his lawyer.

Since only one witness at a time is present at a grand jury hearing, theoretically no witness knows what any other has said or will say. Since there is no practical or legal way to monitor the conversations or phone calls of any of the witnesses called to testify, witnesses can, if they wish, exchange outside the courtroom whatever information they have; they can tell each other what questions were asked and how they answered them. But every attempt is made to keep grand jury testimony secret.

When Newman Flanagan convinced the grand jury to hear testimony he felt would lead to the indictment of Kenneth Edelin, he had already subpoenaed the hospital records of Alice Roe. He knew, as well as could be determined from these records, what people were most likely to have information pertinent to the case.

The grand jury met on February 14, February 21 and again on April 3, 1974. Seventeen witnesses were called, two of them twice. The decisive evidence, the evidence that (in my opinion, having read the grand jury testimony) led to indictment, was that of three doctors—Enrique Giminez, Charles L. Sullivan and George Curtis. (In quoting from their testimo-

74

ny I have not changed errors or inconsistencies in spelling or punctuation. "Doctor," for example, when used alone is sometimes capitalized, sometimes not.)

Dr. Giminez, as you may recall, was the second-year resident who had examined Alice Roe on September 30, the day on which she was admitted to the hospital. At the grand jury investigation he said that when he examined her on that day, it was his opinion, because he was able to feel the top of her uterus four fingerbreadths above the umbilicus, that she was twenty-four weeks pregnant. (One method of estimating length of pregnancy is to feel the top of the uterus through the abdominal wall. At twenty weeks it should be just about at the level of the umbilicus. In succeeding weeks the top climbs above the umbilicus at the rate of one fingerbreadth a week.) Because Alice Roe's pregnancy was so far advanced, he asked one of his senior residents to check her.

Then, he testified, when Alice Roe was admitted to the hospital despite what he felt was a late stage of pregnancy, Giminez—even though Ms. Roe was not his patient—decided to watch the hysterotomy when, eventually, it was performed. He told the grand jury that he watched Dr. Edelin make the incision through the abdomen into the uterus. Then, Giminez said, Edelin reached into the uterus and separated the placenta from the uterine wall. In answer to Flanagan's question "Describe what he [Edelin] did," Giminez said, "He [Edelin] took his hand and pulled the placenta, separated the placenta from the uterus, waited a few minutes and after that he removed the placenta and fetus." (Page 5 of Giminez' February 14 testimony.)

Giminez' testimony as to the time sequence during the hysterotomy is critical. Here are the questions, as asked by Flanagan, and the answers, by Giminez, as recorded in the grand jury minutes:

* * *

Q. Was there a clock in the O.R.?

A. Yes.

Q. What, if anything, after the placenta was removed, what did Dr. Edelin do?

A. He removed the placenta and I think he looked at the clock. [**Note:** Giminez, in this instance, meant "separated" rather than "removed"; his testimony on this point was clarified when he retestified before the grand jury on April 13, 1974.]

Q. Not what you think . . . do you recall whether he looked at the clock?

A. Yes.

Q. For how long a period did he look at the clock?

A. Can't say for sure. . . . Must have been four minutes.

Q. Was it four minutes at least?

A. It was three or four minutes.

Q. And after three or four minutes what did he do?

A. Then he removed the placenta.

Q. You say he removed the placenta first?

A. Yes. The placenta is attached to the uterine cavity and he removed it from the uterine cavity from where it was implanted.

Q. It wasn't connected to the woman at that time?

A. He separated it, that's why he waited.

Q. It was just there on its own? It wasn't connected to the woman?

A. He removed it from where it was attached.

Q. And you say he waited some time and that time was three to four minutes?

A. Yes.

Q. And he watched the clock during that time?

A. Yes.

* * *

So we now have an eyewitness, a doctor who suspected that Alice Roe's fetus might have been alive at the time the hysterotomy was performed, and this witness claims that Dr. Edelin opened the uterus, detached the placenta from the uterus, and then stood and watched a clock for at least three minutes before delivering first the placenta, then the fetus.

What all this meant was explained to the grand jury by Dr. Charles L. Sullivan, a board-certified obstetrician-gynecologist who had at that time been in practice for thirty-five years and had been "associated with some 10,000 pregnancies in private patients." Here are pertinent excerpts from his testimony. The answers are Dr. Sullivan's, the questions—again—from Newman Flanagan. First, a question asked early in the examination.

Q. How does the fetus live? How does it nourish?

A. It depends upon the mother. At the umbilicus, the belly button, is a cord that varies in length and it extends to the placenta. The placenta is a vital organ. That in turn is attached to the mother. And all the nourishment and oxygen goes through the cord to the baby. The reason for the cord is to let the baby float in the fluid. The baby moves *in utero*, practices breathing *in utero*. The baby, placenta and cord are a trio. The mother provides the uterus and nutrient to sustain this baby.

Then, a little later in Dr. Sullivan's testimony, this exchange:

Q. Assuming that you have a fetus that is twenty-four weeks of age or twenty to twenty-eight weeks of age, and assuming further, Doctor, there has twice been a saline injection for the purpose of terminating the fe-

77

tus' life and assuming both times it was unsuccessful and subsequent to that a hysterotomy is performed, and assuming further, Doctor, that after the woman is opened up the placenta is first removed rather than the fetus. Ripped from the mother and taken out. [**Author's note:** This is the only use of the word "rip"—a word I would consider inflammatory—in any of the grand jury testimony.] Assuming that the doctor stands there in the o.r., operating room, and by the clock waits five [sic] minutes before he removes the fetus and when the fetus is removed after that period it is dead, do you have any opinion as to what would cause the death?

A. Yes. First of all the baby survived it's [sic] saline poisoning. Now it's still alive. As you say, it's [sic] source of nourishment and oxygen was threatened. The theoretical doctor took out the placenta first. The supply by which this baby could secure oxygen was removed. The baby would suffocate.

Q. The cause of death would be suffocation?

A. Medically called anoxia. Intrauterine anoxia. If he removed the placenta and left the baby there for five minutes it would succumb to intrauterine anoxia. That baby, by so depriving it of oxygen would struggle to make an effort to breathe. He would try to breathe.

Q. At that time then, the baby is no more dependent upon the mother when the placenta is removed from her womb?

A. It would not depend on the mother anymore.

Q. But it suffocates in the mother's womb?

A. That's right.

Q. Is that standard procedure?

A. Totally not a standard procedure. It's a contrived

78

procedure. It would mean that the doctor was attempting to deprive the baby of life by asphyxiation.

Dr. George Curtis' testimony before the grand jury was to the effect that Alice Roe's baby boy, as best could be determined by weight and measurement, was a viable baby. Dr. Curtis reported that he found no anomalies (unusual features) or defects on either external examination of the baby or on examining its organs. He was not asked about, nor did he volunteer, any information as to what he found on microscopic examination of the fetus.

At the end of his questioning of Dr. Curtis, Newman Flanagan summed up the history of Alice Roe and her pregnancy, asking Dr. Curtis to assume that "there was a hysterotomy performed upon (Alice Roe), the patient, and that at that time the placenta was removed and that the doctor who performed the hysterotomy stood with his hand inside the uterus for a period of three to four minutes; and assuming that after that period of time he removed the fetus, so that the placenta had been removed from the fetus three to four minutes prior to that and when they removed the fetus the fetus was dead. Do you have an opinion doctor, as to the cause of death of that fetus?"

A. I have, in my experience over a long period of years in pathology dealt with fetuses and also with histories. It is my opinion that when the placenta was removed the blood supply from the mother was cut off and no oxygen could get to the baby. The baby does not breathe *in utero*. It's only when they are stimulated to breathe. So the oxygen is cut off from the mother because blood is no longer flowing through the placenta, through the umbilical cord to the fetus. It is a form of asphyxia. Same type of thing if you cut off

79

the air to the lungs you cut off oxygen and that is what keeps you going. If you remove a placenta and leave a baby *in utero* so it can't breathe, that is a form of anoxia or asphyxia.

Q. What would be the cause of death in your opinion?

A. Asphyxia due to anoxia.

Q. In layman's language, that would be suffocation. Death by suffocation?

A. Yes, death by suffocation.

Q. Any questions? Thank you Doctor.

When Dr. Hugh Holtrop was called to testify, he refused, on the advice of his attorney, to answer any questions with regard to the Alice Roe case. As Dr. Holtrop told me later, "In my opinion, Dr. Edelin would have been wise to do the same." But Dr. Edelin's attorney (whom he later dropped when he retained attorney Bill Homans) apparently did not advise him against testifying. So when Newman Flanagan asked him to describe the hysterotomy, which he readily admitted he had done on Alice Roe, he answered. Here are Flanagan's questions and Dr. Edelin's responses.

Q. Tell us how you did it [the hysterotomy]. What procedure was used on this particular case?

A. Routine procedure. After the abdomen is opened a very small incision is made into the uterus and what you attempt to do is keep the amniotic fluid, it's within the uterus, the fetus and lining of the uterus, from spilling over into the abdominal cavity and I attempt to deliver everything intact, by putting your finger inside the uterus and sweeping around and separate the placenta and remove it on-block.

Q. Did you do that in this particular instance?

A. That is the usual procedure and whether I did it in this particular case I don't know.

Newman Flanagan did not ask Dr. Edelin how long it had taken him to perform the hysterotomy or whether he had, as Giminez had testified, separated the placenta from the uterus and then kept the detached fetus in the uterus for three minutes while he watched a clock. Nor did Dr. Edelin volunteer any information on these points, presumably because he didn't know what other witnesses had said.

Dr. Edelin did say that he estimated the fetal age at twenty weeks. He did not believe the fetus was alive when he removed it since, to his recollection, he had never delivered a live fetus at hysterotomy. He did not know who had signed the death certificate. That was, Dr. Edelin said, "the function of staff people."

After hearing the testimony of all the witnesses Newman Flanagan chose to call, the members of the grand jury voted to indict Dr. Kenneth Edelin for manslaughter. Having read the testimony, I am sure I would also have voted to indict.

9

Let me reemphasize here that Dr. Edelin was not being brought to trial because he had performed an abortion. The Supreme Court decision was clear. During the first trimester (the first twelve weeks) of pregnancy, the state could not restrict a woman's right to an abortion. During the second trimester, from the twelfth to the twenty-fourth week, the only restrictions the state might impose were those designed to protect the life and well-being of the mother. Only in pregnancies that were beyond the twenty-fourth week might the state consider the fetus as "viable" and restrict or even deny a woman's right to abortion.

However, the Supreme Court did not say what ought or must be done if a live fetus resulted from the abortion. Since the point of an abortion is to rid a woman of an unwanted pregnancy, many would argue that it is unreasonable to work to save the life of an unwanted fetus who will, in all probability, die unless strenuous efforts are made to save its life. Others argue that if the fetus is born alive, the doctor has an

William A. Nolen, M.D.

obligation to try to keep it alive. In most hospitals, among
them Boston City Hospital, it is supposedly the practice of the
medical staff to try to sustain the life of a live-born aborted fetus. (A fetus is considered to be alive if it demonstrates any
one of four things: (1) movement of arms or legs, (2) breathing, (3) a hearbeat or (4) pulsation of the umbilical cord which
would be considered evidence of a fetal heartbeat. I suspect
that the attempts to sustain the lives of aborted fetuses are often not very vigorous or enthusiastic.)

Edelin was accused of actually killing a child; as the indictment read, "[Kenneth Edelin] did assault and beat a certain
person, to wit, a male child described to the said jurors as
'baby boy' and by such assault and beating did kill said person."

The indictment is not, of course, to be taken literally. No
one claimed that Dr. Edelin delivered a live baby and then
beat it with his hands or a club. The indictment is simply a legal definition of manslaughter. It was the contention of the
district attorney that when Kenneth Edelin opened Alice
Roe's uterus he found a live baby and that he then tried to kill
that baby by asphyxiating it. To repeat: Kenneth Edelin was
being tried for manslaughter, not for abortion.

After his indictment, Dr. Edelin changed lawyers. He hired
attorney William Homans to defend him. As Homans told me,
"I was sitting in my office one afternoon when the phone
rang. I answered it, and the guy identified himself as Dr.
Kenneth Edelin. He asked me if I'd represent him. I hadn't
been following the medical cases except casually, but I knew
there were two trials pending. I said 'Are you one of the
grave-robber doctors or are you the manslaughter case?' 'I'm
the manslaughter case,' Ken said. So I said, 'Fine, I'll defend
you.' I'd have probably taken the grave-robber case if it came
my way, but I preferred the manslaughter case. It seemed to
me, even though I didn't know much about it, that it would be
more clear-cut than the other."

84

Bill Homans is in his middle fifties, about six feet tall, weighs 190 pounds and usually looks rumpled. His features are best described as "craggy"—blunt, big nose and jaw, large hands, a sort of roughhewn Abe Lincoln type.

His reputation as a lawyer suits his appearance. "He sleeps in his office about half the time," my brother Jim, who is also a lawyer, told me. "At least that's his reputation. He's also supposed to be a top-notch defense lawyer. He's always taking on these cases that are tough to win—defending hoodlums who have mugged old people, that sort of stuff. Those kind of cases don't often pay much so he also has the reputation of being anything but wealthy. But everybody—the judges who sit on his cases, the opposing lawyers, even the DA and his staff—seems to like him."

When I met and talked with Homans, as I did several times in the course of investigating the Edelin case, he was always cordial, and, though I knew he was a very busy man, he never hurried me. He answered all my questions fully and went out of his way to get papers that he thought might be helpful to me.

He is, as my brother told me, an avid tennis player. I was with him in his office one evening at about five P.M. when he called a friend to try to arrange a tennis match for seven the next morning. "Call me back," he said to the man. "Yeah, I'm home. I'm in my office. That's home to me."

"Do you always play that early in the morning?" I asked.

"Usually," he said. "I've got to be in court at nine tomorrow. Tonight I'm playing doubles at nine-thirty. We'll probably play for a couple of hours if no one else has the court."

"You must be in pretty good shape," I said.

"Not too bad," he said, "and I'm trying to stay that way. You probably don't know, but at the time the Edelin trial ended I weighed about 230 pounds—I'm forty pounds lighter now—and I was really in rotten shape. In fact, this story might interest you. The weekend after the trial I decided to

85

take a couple of days off to go skiing up in Vermont. I had the car radio on and I was sort of half listening to one of these guys who was being interviewed about heart attacks. He was instructing his audience on how to tell a heart attack from a muscle strain.

"I skied all weekend and then Monday when I was back in the office, about ten in the morning, I noticed a little soreness in my chest on the left side. I figured it was probably a muscle strain but after an hour it was not only still there, it was beginning to go into my left shoulder. Naturally, I began to wonder if it could be a heart attack.

"One of the things I remembered from the radio talk was that alcohol often relieved heart pain even though it didn't do anything for muscle pain. So I left the office for a few minutes, walked across the street to the Parker House and had a couple of quick shots of Jack Daniels. About half an hour after I got back to the office, the pain went away, so I figured maybe it was a heart attack. In fact, a client called me just about then—it was around 11:30—and wanted to set up a meeting for that afternoon. I told him to call me back at two and I'd see him if I was here, but I might not be because I thought I was having a heart attack."

Let me interject here that as Homans told me this story there wasn't a flicker of a smile on his face. He was puffing away on True cigarettes, which he chain smokes, lighting one from the butt of another, and talking very seriously.

"Anyway," he continued, "I said to my secretary, 'I think I'm having a heart attack. I'm going down to the General [The Massachusetts General Hospital, just a few blocks from Homans' office]. If it's not a heart attack, I'll be back soon. Otherwise, I'll call you.' So I got in a cab and went to the General.

"When I got there, I remembered I owed them about ninety dollars on an old bill. I thought it would be embarrassing to be admitted with an old bill outstanding, so I started looking around for the office where I could pay up. As I was wander-

ing around a young intern came up to me—he must have recognized me because my picture had been in the Boston papers a lot the last week—and he said 'Can I do something for you, Mr. Homans?'

"I told him, 'I think I'm having a heart attack, but before I see anyone I want to get my bill paid. Where do I go to pay up?' 'Just wait there,' the kid said, and in about thirty seconds he came back to me pushing a wheelchair.

"Well, I tell you, I've never really been afraid of dying, but I've always dreaded being disabled. The sight of that wheelchair just scared the daylights out of me. As soon as I saw it I keeled right over in a faint, and when I came to, I was up in the intensive care unit hooked up to all kinds of wires and tubes. I was having a heart attack, and I was in that hospital for three weeks. I lost some weight there, some more when I got out, and I'm planning to stay right at 190 where I am now, and I'm going to take life easy and stay in shape. I don't want any more heart attacks.

"I try not to let things bother me. My cases still get to me once in a while, but I don't let my social life—I've had some family problems—get me all excited. I try to keep things under control."

That night we had dinner with a woman friend of Bill's at seven. She kept trying—unsuccessfullly—to keep him from chain smoking. After dinner he left to play tennis. Fortunately, I thought, he'd eaten a fairly light meal, since it isn't wise to exercise vigorously after a heavy meal. He had with him a briefcase full of papers he planned to read after that night's tennis match, in preparation for the case he'd try the next day after his seven A.M. singles match.

I could only wonder what his schedule must have been like before he decided to take life easy and stay in shape.

At other times, in conversations with the lawyers from the district attorney's office, I never heard anything but good about Bill Homans. He was not only respected but liked, even

87

by the lawyers who fought with him in the courtroom. As one of them told me, "He's a hell of a nice guy and a damn good lawyer. And one other thing—he can sure drink. I've seen him knock off half a dozen martinis, one right after the other, and you wouldn't know he'd had anything more than a glass of water. He's an amazing man."

Since its relevance in the case was, later, a matter of dispute, I may as well mention here that Kenneth Edelin is a black man. Edelin is about 5'8", stocky but not fat, has black hair and a mustache and a complexion I would call lighter than Mediterranean. He is, in fact, a white black man.

We will discuss the relevance or irrelevance of his color later, but certainly it was not a factor in bringing the indictment against him. Newman Flanagan told me, "I was shocked when I learned, long after I'd first seen him, that he was black. I don't remember exactly how I found out—I think it was from a newspaper story—but I do remember going to Garrett and saying, 'Damn it, Garrett, Edelin is black.' He wasn't any happier than I was. We knew that, with the busing issue still hot here in Boston, we'd run into cries of 'racism' before the trial was over."

Bill Homans told me a similar story. "I was wondering why we were getting so much support from the black community. It seemed odd to me. It wasn't until after I'd met with Ken two or three times that I learned he was black."

One of the first decisions Homans had to make was whether to try the case before a judge alone or to ask for a jury trial. Judge James P. McGuire had been assigned the case. After deliberation and some research, Homans decided on a jury.

"I had nothing personal against Judge McGuire," Homans told me. "He had been a prosecutor at one time. But he was a Catholic, and we learned that he had received awards from the Pope and from various Catholic organizations. We knew

there would be enormous pressure put on him by the Catholic community. I had no doubt he would be fair, but still we decided we had a better chance with a jury. So that's the way we went."

The next decision Homans had to make was whether or not to ask for a change of venue. Could he be certain of getting a fair trial in predominantly Catholic Boston, particularly in view of the busing controversy and the antiblack feeling it had engendered?

"Before we made that decision, we ran a poll. It cost us some money, but money wasn't a major concern—there were donations coming in from all across the country for the Kenneth Edelin defense fund. In fact, this has been one of those rare cases where I've been able to charge decent lawyer fees and collect.

"If you ask for a change of venue and it's granted, you get whatever county the luck of the draw gives you; it's chosen at random. After our poll was taken it seemed to me that the only two counties that might be an improvement on Suffolk were Nantucket or Duke County. Otherwise, Suffolk was probably as good as or better than any other place in Massachusetts. We decided to stay here. I felt we'd get a fair trial."

The results of the poll, done by the Decision Research Corporation of Wellesley Hills, Massachusetts were not very surprising. Those polled were prospective jurors; i.e., residents of Suffolk County between the ages of eighteen and sixty-nine. College students, doctors, hospital patients and any others who would be legally excluded from jury duty were not questioned. Of the prospective jurors 56 percent were Catholic, reflecting the religious composition of Suffolk County. Fifteen percent of all those polled said they believed it was always wrong to perform an abortion, but when asked if they believed it was wrong if having a baby might be dangerous to the mother's physical or mental health, the 15 percent dropped to 9 percent.

The other pertinent factors the poll revealed were these:

(1) People over fifty were more strongly antiabortion than were the young.

(2) Most of those polled felt that abortion after the fifth month of pregnancy was wrong; generally, first trimester abortions were not as strongly opposed.

(3) The greater the person's annual income, the less likely he or she was to be antiabortion. For example, 23 percent of those with incomes below $5,000 were strongly antiabortion; if annual income was over $25,000, only 4 percent were antiabortion. Similarly, the more education a person had, the less likely they were to be strongly antiabortion.

(4) People who had adopted or tried to adopt children were likely to be strongly antiabortion.

(5) Those who regularly read the *Pilot*, the Catholic newspaper of the Suffolk County diocese, were likely to be strongly antiabortion, as were those Catholics who had gone to parochial school.

(6) Of those who felt that abortion in the sixth month of pregnancy was wrong (62 percent), most (84 percent) felt that they could disregard their personal prejudices, listen to the evidence and approach the case with an open mind.

(7) Finally—and this was for Homans and Edelin the bottom line—11 percent said that where abortion took place during the sixth month they would be likely to find the defendant guilty even if the judge instructed them that abortions performed before the end of the sixth month were legal. The percentage was almost the same (9 percent) if the abortion took place during the fifth month.

With the results of the poll at hand, Homans knew the type of juror to avoid—a poor Catholic, over fifty, who was a parochial school dropout and read the *Pilot* regularly. He also knew what sort of questions to ask (e.g., "If the defendant performed an abortion on a woman who was twenty weeks pregnant, will you feel obligated to find him guilty even if the

judge tells you such an abortion is legal?") to keep off the jury that 11 percent who simply could not give his client a fair trial.

On Monday, January 6, 1975, when the court assembled to begin proceedings, Homans' first move was to try to get the case dismissed on grounds that the grand jury which had indicted Kenneth Edelin was not chosen from a representative panel of jurors. Nor, he contended, were the members of the panel from which the jurors for this case were to be selected a representative group.

The problem was one of sex discrimination. In 1974 the city of Boston, in selecting a panel from which to choose jurors, programmed its computer so that there would be two males for every female in the group from which jurors would eventually be selected. This had resulted, in the grand jury of 18 which indicted Kenneth Edelin, in a male to female ratio of 14:4. Of the 150 people from whom the jury for Edelin's trial were to be selected, 131 came from Boston, the other 19 from smaller cities in Suffolk County. In the smaller cities the potential jurors were chosen in a way that would provide an even sexual distribution. But of the 131 potential jurors from Boston, 99 were males and only 32 were females, a ratio greater than 3:1.

Newman Flanagan pointed out that Boston was gradually approaching a fifty-fifty ratio in its male to female juror selection process; that only a few years earlier the ratio had been six males to every female. Homans argued that though this was very nice, it was of no help to his client, who was being denied the unbiased juror selection process the Constitution guaranteed him. Judge McGuire refused to accept the male-female bias as grounds for dismissal. He decided it would be possible to find an unbiased group of 16 jurors from among the 150 individuals who had been called for jury duty.

Next, before the jury was selected, Homans reviewed with

91

the judge the findings of the poll. He asked Judge McGuire to conduct a *voir dire*, i.e., an individual interrogation of each juror, to make certain he or she did not fall into the category of the 11 percent who, presumably, would find Kenneth Edelin guilty of manslaughter simply because he had performed an abortion in the fifth or sixth month. Judge McGuire agreed. Here, from the trial transcript (pp. 3-88 through 3-104), are two consecutive examples of the interrogations carried out by Judge McGuire:

Paul T. Kolesinski, sworn examination by the court:

Q. Now, sir, give me your name and address?
A. Paul T. Kolesinski.
Q. Do a lot better than that.
A. Paul Kolesinski; 16 Vinton Street, South Boston, Mass.
Q. Now, you were here yesterday, were you, when I talked to the jury?
A. Yes, I was.
Q. Are you aware of any physical or personal problem that would interfere with your serving as a juror having in mind that this case will last four or five weeks and the jury will be locked up?
A. No.
Q. Now, what is your occupation?
A. I am a shipwright in the Boston Naval Shipyard.
Q. Married or single?
A. Married.
Q. Of how many does your family consist?
A. Wife and a daughter.
Q. How old is the daughter?
A. Eight.
Q. Does your wife work?
A. No, she doesn't.

92

Q. This is the trial of Kenneth Edelin who has been indicted for manslaughter.

He was a resident of Harrison Avenue in Boston and is now a resident of Cambridge.

Do you know him or are you related to him?

A. No.

Q. The attorneys in the case are Mr. Flanagan, Mr. Mulligan, Mr. Dunn and Mr. Brennan for the Commonwealth. And Mr. Homans and Mr. Susman for the defendant. The defendant is sitting at Mr. Homans' left.

Are you related to or do you know any of them?

A. No, I don't.

Q. Are you related to or do you have any close association with any law enforcement officer?

A. Well, I know some, yes.

Q. Do you have any close association with any of them?

A. Well, I have a relative that is a state trooper.

Q. What relationship?

A. A cousin.

Q. Well, that wouldn't interfere, would it, with your forming a fair and impartial judgment in this case?

A. I have no idea.

Q. No idea? Well, it wouldn't, would it?

A. No, not really, no.

Q. I don't mean to be impolite.

A. No; I misunderstood.

Q. You would form your own opinion, wouldn't you?

A. Sure.

Q. Do you have any relative or close associate in the District Attorney's office?

A. No, I haven't.

Q. Do you have any relationship with or close association with anyone at the Boston City Hospital in the obstetrical or gynecological department?

93

A. No, I don't.

Q. Now, do you have any personal interest in this case?

A. Not really, no.

Q. Have you read anything in the newspapers, seen anything on television, heard anything on the radio or read any journals, national or local in scope and distribution, magazines or periodicals, having to do with this case?

A. Yes, last week.

Q. What was it?

A. I didn't go through the whole thing. I just seen the—

Q. Newspaper or magazine?

A. Newspaper. I just seen it in the newspaper and scanned through it.

Q. Did you form any opinion about the merits of the case?

A. I didn't read the whole thing.

Q. Well, no matter how much you read, did you form an opinion?

A. No, not really, no.

Q. Now, could you in good conscience form a fair and impartial and candid judgment based upon the evidence you would hear if you are a juror in this case and the charge of the Court as to the law, uninfluenced by anything else?

A. I really couldn't say. I doubt it very much.

Q. You doubt that you could?

A. Yes.

Q. Are you saying to me that you have an opinion about abortions? Is that what you are saying?

A. I don't know anything about them, really.

Q. Well, do you have an opinion as to whether they are right or wrong?

A. I think they are wrong, yes.

Q. Well, under our system of government, the jurors hear the facts in a case, they hear the testimony, and the jurors are the sole judges of the facts as determined from the testimony and the exhibits and the stipulations that are made in the Court. Then the jurors are obliged to accept the law as the Court gives it to them, the law that's applicable to that case, whether you particularly agree with that law or not.

A. All right.

Q. Now, based on those two things, the evidence and the charge, would you be able to form a fair and impartial opinion and judgment about this case, uninfluenced by anything else?

A. I think I could if I heard the case, yes. I don't know the case.

Q. You don't know anything about it, do you?

A. No.

Q. I say suppose you were sitting down there in one of the jury seats, and you heard the testimony, attentively listened to it all, and you heard the charge that the Court gives about what law is applicable to it, could you form a fair and impartial judgment based solely on those two things, as to the guilt or innocence of this defendant?

A. I think so, yes.

Q. Are you a member of any religious group or sect or association, the membership in which would influence you or tend to influence you in reaching a decision in this case?

A. No.

Q. Do you belong to any organization or association which has expressed an opinion concerning abortions?

A. No.

William A. Nolen, M.D.

Q. Have you heard any expression of views by any religious personage or anybody else in regard to this case or in reference to abortions?
A. No.
Q. Read that to yourself. (This was a list that contained the names of probable witnesses.)
A. (Juror complies.)
Q. Have you read those names?
A. Yes.
Q. Do you know anyone whose name appears thereon?
A. No.
Q. This juror stands indifferent.
Mr. Flanagan: The Commonwealth is content with this juror, your Honor.
The Defendant: I accept this juror, your Honor.
Paul T. Kolesinski, Juror No. 6

The Clerk: No. 92, Mary F. Malinowski.
Mary F. Malinowski, sworn examination by the court:
Q. I am going to ask you your name and address.
A. Mary F. Malinowski, 875 East Broadway, South Boston, Mass.
Q. A little louder, if you can?
A. Say it again?
Q. No. You were here yesterday when I spoke to you, were you?
A. Yes.
Q. As a group?
A. Yes.
Q. Are you aware of any physical or personal problem that would interfere with you serving as a juror having in mind that this trial will last four or five weeks and that the jury will be locked up?

A. Well, I am expecting our first grandchild any day this month, and I would like to be there.

Q. Your presence isn't necessary, is it?

A. No, I don't think so.

Q. Anything else?

A. But I would like to be there.

Q. Well, I appreciate that. But I cannot accept that as a reason, unfortunately.

There is no harm in telling you.

A. No.

Q. Anything else that would prevent you from being a juror?

A. No, I don't think so.

Q. Now, what is your occupation?

A. I work in a meat plant, pickling hams. We cure the hams.

Q. Curing hams?

A. Yes.

Q. For whom do you work?

A. Colonial Provision, Inc.

Q. Are you married or single?

A. I am married.

Q. Does your husband work?

A. Yes.

Q. Where?

A. At Brink's, Inc.

Q. Brink's?

A. Yes.

Q. What is he—a guard?

A. Yes.

Q. Now, this is the trial of Kenneth Edelin who has been indicted for manslaughter.

The defendant was a resident of Harrison Avenue in Boston and is now a resident of Cambridge.

97

William A. Nolen, M.D.

Are you related to or do you know him?

A. No, I don't know him.

Q. The attorneys in the case are Mr. Flanagan, Mr. Mulligan, Mr. Dunn and Mr. Brennan. They are attorneys for the Commonwealth.

Mr. Homans and Mr. Susman are for the defendant, and the defendant is sitting at Mr. Homans' left.

Are you related or do you know any of them?

A. No, I don't think so.

Q. Are you related or do you have any close association with any law enforcement officer?

A. No.

Q. Are you related or do you have any close association with anyone in the District Attorney's office?

A. No.

Q. Are you related or do you have any close association with any employee of the Boston City Hospital in the obstetrics and gynecology department?

A. No.

Q. Do you have any personal interest in this case?

A. No, not really.

Q. Well, have you read anything in the newspapers, heard anything on the radio, seen anything on TV or read any magazines or journals or periodicals, whether they be national in scope or local in scope and distribution, having anything to do with the defendant or with this case?

A. Well, I read Monday's paper.

Q. What did you read?

A. That the trial was supposed to start today and they were going to pick the jury.

Q. Anything else besides that that you read?

A. And my daughter said, "Oh, ma, you are going on that case."

98

Q. Neither of those things caused you to form any opinion about it, did they?

A. Well, no, not really.

Q. No, you just read that the case was coming up and your daughter said you will be called?

A. Yes.

Q. Now, is it fair to say that you do not have any impression of the guilt or innocence of the defendant at this time?

A. Yes.

Q. Now, could you, if you sat as a juror, form a fair and impartial opinion, render a fair and impartial opinion in this case based solely on the testimony and the evidence that you accept in court and the charge as to the law that I give to you?

A. Yes, I think I could.

Q. Let me ask you this: Are you conscious of any bias or prejudice in relation to this case?

A. No.

Q. Have you formed or expressed any opinion as to the guilt or innocence of the defendant?

A. No.

Q. Do you have an opinion as to whether or not abortions are wrong?

A. Well, they are.

Q. Tell me what your opinion is?

A. Well, I don't believe, really, in them.

Q. Well, in our system of trying cases and hearing cases you listen to the evidence of the witnesses, the testimony of the witnesses, and you accept the law as the Court gives it to you, regardless of whether you think that law is correct or not, regardless of whether you might like to change it.

You have to accept the applicable law in the instant case as the Court gives it to you.

Now, could you based on those two things, listening, return a fair and impartial judgment in this case, even though the law as I give it to you may not be what you like it to be or may not be what you understand it now to be?

Could you render a fair and impartial judgment?

A. I don't know.

Q. Well, this is the time to find out, right now. You've got to be frank and fair. You have an obligation as a citizen to be a juror. You've got to be a fair juror.

A. Well, I would try. I don't know—

Q. Well, you've got to be frank.

Could you listen to the testimony in the case and listen to me tell you what the law is and accept it and say, "Yes, I accept the law as the Judge gives it to us, and I'll form my judgment and return a verdict based on that?"

A. Yes.

Q. Are you a member of any religious group or sect or association, the membership in which would influence you or tend to influence you in reaching a decision in this case?

A. Well, I am Catholic, yes.

Q. You are a Catholic.

Now, I ask you, as a member of the Catholic Church, do you feel that your being a member of the Catholic Church would influence you or tend to influence you in reaching a decision in the case based, as I have said, upon the testimony in the case and the charge as to the law that I will give you?

A. No.

Q. No what?

A. No, it wouldn't.

Q. It wouldn't?

A. No.

100

Q. Now, do you, aside from your membership in the church, belong to any organization or association, which association or organization has expressed opinions concerning abortions?

A. No.

Q. Have you heard any expression of views by any religious personage or by any other person which would influence you or tend to influence you in reference to this case?

A. No.

Q. Read this to yourself.

A. (Juror complies.) Yes.

Q. Do you know anyone whose names are on that card?

A. No.

Q. All right.

Mr. Homans: May I approach the bench?

The Court: Yes, you may.

(Bench conference not recorded.)

The Court: I am going to ask you one more question:

Q. In view of your opinion or belief as to abortions would you be able to approach the evidence in this case and form a fair and unbiased opinion thereon and accept the instructions as given to you by the Court as to the law that's applicable?

A. No, I don't believe in abortions.

Q. Well, I didn't ask you that. You've expressed your opinion that you have no belief.

A. Well, I will try.

Q. I appreciate your answer that you would try. But I've got to delve into it a little more precisely.

In view of your opinion or belief as to abortion would you be able to approach the evidence in this case and form a fair and unbiased opinion thereon and accept the instructions as given you by the Court as to the law?

A. No, I don't think so.

Q. Why not? You say you don't think so.

A. I don't know. I don't know what the case is about.

The Court: I know you don't. No one knows what this case is about—not until we hear—

A. I don't know how I would act.

Q. I am not asking you how you would act. I am asking you, in your mind, if you feel, having in mind the opinion which you have openly and honestly told me about abortion—do you feel that you would be able to approach the evidence in the case, listen to it, and to listen to the Court as to what the law is, and based on those two things, and those two things alone, form a fair and unbiased opinion in regard to this case?

A. No, I don't think so.

The Court: Excused for cause.

(Juror excused.)

The Court: I'll see counsel.

(Bench conference not recorded.)

Along with the jurors excused for "cause," i.e., because Judge McGuire decided the person would not be an accepted juror for reasons of health, family or work obligation or (as in the case of Mary Malinowski) because she could not promise to give an unbiased opinion—the prosecutor and the defense were each allowed eight peremptory challenges. A peremptory challenge is one in which a juror is refused without giving any specific reason. These peremptory challenges allow the attorneys for both sides to use their experience and instinct to decide which people, despite their claims of objectivity, may be subtly prejudiced in either direction.

Ordinarily, in a manslaughter trial, each side is allowed only four peremptory challenges. Homans had asked for sixteen

peremptory challenges in this case—a number equal to that of the jurors empaneled—but McGuire had compromised at eight. As it turned out, neither prosecution nor defense used all the challenges allotted them.

Juries are eventually reduced to twelve people. In major trials, extra persons—sometimes making a total of fourteen or sixteen—act as jurors through the trial. Then if one or two have to be excused for illness or some other reason before the trial is finished, there are still twelve left to deliberate and reach a verdict.

In most states if extra jurors are still in attendance at the time the trial ends and deliberations begin, the last jurors chosen are dismissed. In Massachusetts the jurors to be dismissed are chosen by lot. The only person on the jury who is not subject to dismissal is the foreman. The foreman is chosen by the judge after all the jurors have been selected, but before the trial begins.

Of the sixteen jurors chosen to hear the Edelin case, three were women and thirteen were men. The foreman, Vincent Shea, was a mechanic, married, with four daughters ranging in age from nine to eighteen.

After the jury selection, but before the trial began, Homans and Flanagan agreed that the name of the young woman who had undergone the abortion would not be used. Neither side felt it would be necessary to call her to testify, and so they chose to preserve her anonymity.

They did argue, before Judge McGuire but not before the jury, as to what terminology would be used in referring to the supposed victim of the manslaughter. Homans insisted the only suitable word was "fetus." Flanagan felt he and his witnesses should be allowed to refer to the victim as "male child," though he preferred "baby boy." Here is an excerpt from their discussion (pp. 5-6 to 5-8):

* * *

103

The Court: Tell me again what your position is about the use of the words "baby boy."

Mr. Flanagan: "Baby boy" is the word that is actually in the indictment. The jury is going to read the indictment. The Commonwealth will introduce evidence, or hopefully will do so, that the deceased is a baby boy. The medical examiner has already described it as a baby boy in his autopsy report, and the Commonwealth will introduce evidence to that effect.

The Court: I will you on that, Mr. Homans.

Mr. Homans: May it please the Court, under the decison in Roe against Wade, and under other applicable decisions, may it please the Court, considering the baby boy as the earliest kind of male human being. I would suggest, your Honor, that there is no evidence, and that there will be no evidence that this fetus ever breathed, as the Commonwealth's evidence will indicate, and that therefore it never became a human being, ergo, not a baby boy, and I would object to the use of those words.

The Court: I will allow the words "human being" or "male human being" to be used, and deny your motion other than as has been indicated, and save the defendant's exceptions.

Mr. Homans: Thank you, your Honor.

(Exception No. 1.)

Mr. Flanagan: What did you say on "baby boy?"

The Court: I said you will not use the words "baby boy," but you may use the words "human being," or "male human being," or "male child." Otherwise, the motion is denied, and the defendant's exception is saved.

They also argued over the words suffocate, smother and murder, all of which Flanagan thought were appropriate; Homans felt that none of them should be used. Judge McGuire finally decided, "In view of counsel's statement that he in-

tends and expects to introduce evidence as to the generally accepted meaning of anoxia as including suffocation, I will allow him to use that word. I will not allow you to use the word 'smother' or 'murder.' ''

The preliminary skirmishes over, on Friday, January 10, 1975, the indictment was read to the jury and the trial began.

10

The opening witness for the prosecution was Dr. Mildred Jefferson, the same Dr. Jefferson who had testified at Dapper O'Neil's open hearings. She is a handsome black woman and a 1951 graduate of Harvard Medical School. A board-certified general surgeon, she is an assistant clinical professor of surgery at Boston University School of Medicine. Particulary pertinent, as far as this case was concerned, is the fact that Dr. Jefferson was (and is) extremely active in most if not all the Right-to-Life movements. As she said in the course of her direct examination by attorney Joseph Mulligan, an assistant to Newman Flanagan, "I am a founding member of all such organizations represented in Massachusetts, beginning with the education organization known as the Value of Life Committee, and the political education organization known as Massachusetts Citizens for Life. Both organizations are dedicated to providing some balanced and sound information in the public discussion, and to defend the sanctity of life, I think, as the basis of a democratic society." (Homans moved

that the last part of this statement be deleted as having no relevance and being prejudicial. The judge allowed it to stand.)

Dr. Jefferson had ostensibly been called as a witness just so that she could explain the process of conception, development and birth and define medical terms to be used during the trial. It would seem apparent that an obstetrician-gynecologist rather than a general surgeon would have been the logical specialist to do this job. Dr. Jefferson was probably chosen because (1) she had spoken about abortion many times to large groups of lay people and would know how to simplify medical terminology so the jury could understand it; (2) she was a black and would help the state avert any cry of "racism" for prosecuting Edelin; (3) she was a woman, which would help erase any idea that this was a trial in which men were fighting against the right of women to control their bodies. She seemed an excellent choice as the first witness for the prosecution.

Between the day when Mildred Jefferson took the stand—Friday, January 10, 1975—and Tuesday, February 18, 1975, when the trial was concluded, there were over four thousand pages of testimony by dozens of witnesses. Interspersed were many objections—most of them by the defense—to testimony, terminology and legal proceedings. Having reviewed all this material—and having discussed most of the disputed matters with both Bill Homans and Newman Flanagan—I shall summarize the case, emphasizing both the areas of agreement and dispute.

First, a review of the anatomy and physiology of pregnancy. The reproductive cycle of a woman, from the first day of one menstrual period to the first day of the next, may run anywhere from twenty-one to thirty-five days. The average is about twenty-eight days. In most women, whatever the length of her cycle, it is usually constant, not varying more than one or two days each month. However, stress, either emotional or

physical, may cause a change in her usual rhythm. It is relatively common, for example, for a woman who fears she is pregnant and does not want to be pregnant to have her menstrual period arrive a few days or even a few weeks late. Fear is a form of stress.

Most women ovulate a few days before the middle of their cycle. A woman with a twenty-one-day cycle may ovulate around the fifth day; with a twenty-eight-day cycle she will probably ovulate around the twelfth day. The ovum, or egg, then enters the fallopian tube, a hollow tube about five inches in length and about a half inch in circumference that extends out from the upper portion of each side of the uterus. The ovum, if it is not fertilized, passes down the tube into the uterus and then is shed along with the inner lining of the uterus at the time of the next menstrual period.

If, however, the woman has intercourse any time from just before to a few days after ovulation, some of the millions of sperm that are contained in the semen may make their way up into the uterus and out into the fallopian tube where one may penetrate the ovum, fertilizing it. The fertilized ovum is known as a zygote. The zygote divides into two cells, then four and then keeps dividing as it travels toward the uterus. The trip down the fallopian tube into the uterus takes somewhere between six and eight days, by which time the fertilized ovum has become a mass of cells known as a blastula. The blastula burrows into the wall of the uterus about nine days after fertilization has taken place. Once this multicelled structure is buried in the wall of the uterus, it is known as an embryo. The embryo, as its cells continue to multiply, develops connections with the blood vessels in the wall of the mother's uterus. These connections will eventually become a disc-shaped structure known as the placenta.

Generally, once fertilization has occurrred and the embryo is embedded in the wall of the mother's uterus, her menstrual periods will cease. Sometimes, however, particularly at the

time the embryo is burrowing into the inner lining of the uterus, there will be a little bleeding from the uterus. A woman may mistake this for her normal menstrual period. She is particularly apt to make this error if she does not want to be pregnant but is afraid she may be. The fact that the embryo works itself into the uterine wall just about at the time a normal menstrual period might be expected adds to the possibility that the woman will deceive herself. Rarely, a woman will have slight bleeding—pseudo-menstrual periods—almost every month through her pregnancy.

When the embryo is embedded in the uterus and has formed a connection with the mother through the placenta, the nourishment of the embryo as it continues to grow comes from the mother's blood. Waste products from the embryo will flow into the mother's bloodstream, and she will excrete them through her kidneys, lungs and bowel. As the embryo grows, the cells differentiate and arrange themselves into organs. About eight weeks after fertilization, most of the organs that will be part of the adult body—the kidneys, the heart, the eye, the genitalia—are rudimentary but recognizable, and some are functioning. By this time, i.e., at about eight weeks, the embryo will be floating in fluid enclosed in a thin-walled sac; the sac is called the amniotic sac and the fluid is amniotic fluid. At this stage of development the nomenclature again shifts and the embryo becomes known as a fetus.

The fetus remains attached to the uterus by a cord that runs between the placenta and the umbilicus of the fetus. This umbilical cord consists of blood vessels—veins and arteries—coated by a rubbery, gelatinous substance. It looks like a plastic tube that at the time of a normal birth is about one inch in diameter and about twenty inches long. The fetus continues to receive its nourishment from the mother through the vein that runs from the placenta inside the umbilical cord and on into the fetus. Waste products are pumped back by the fetal heart along the umbilical arteries to the placenta and then on into

110

the mother's bloodstream to be excreted, eventually, by her organs. As long as it is in the mother's uterus, the fetus will depend on her bloodstream to bring it all the nutrients and oxygen it needs not only to survive but to grow and mature. Late in pregnancy the fetus will swallow amniotic fluid and excrete it; it will also breathe amniotic fluid in and out of its lungs. But the amniotic fluid will not supply the fetus either with nourishment or oxygen.

An average pregnancy, as previously mentioned, lasts 266 days from the time fertilization takes place till the time the woman goes into labor and the baby is delivered. However, even if the woman has had intercourse only once during the month she becomes pregnant, and so knows exactly when the impregnating sperm entered her uterus, she still cannot be exactly certain on which day fertilization takes place. Since the ovum requires about a week to pass through the fallopian tube, and since the sperm retains its ability to fertilize the ovum for about forty-eight hours, fertilization may take place any time during the seventy-two hours after intercourse. It may also occur at either the far end of the tube or closer to the uterus, and on both these factors will depend the exact date when normal delivery of the fully developed baby will occur. In fact, according to one of the standard obstetrical textbooks, in trying to determine "Expected Date of Confinement"—the "E.D.C." or "due date"—if you know the date of fruitful coitus and count forward 266 days, in "about one half of the cases this date will be accurate within seven days." Since it is only in the exceptional case that one knows the actual date of fruitful coitus—and since this, the most accurate method of determining length of pregnancy, leaves room for a two-week margin of error—it follows that any other system of determining duration of pregnancy is probably not going to allow for any greater accuracy. This is, in fact, the case.

From the practical point of view most obstetricians, when predicting a patient's due date, apply what is known as "Na-

William A. Nolen, M.D.

gele's rule." This rule states that if you count back three months from the first day of the woman's last menstrual period and add one week, you will know approximately when her baby is due.

According to the hospital records, when Alice Roe reported her menstrual history to Dr. Hugh Holtrop on September 21, 1973, she said that her last menstrual period had begun on May 28, 1973. If this were in fact the case, then, Dr. Holtrop figured, Alice's due date would be March 7. (May 28 minus three months would be February 28; adding one week would bring her to March 7.) Or, to figure it in the other direction, if her last menstrual period was on May 28, then she probably got pregnant on or about June 14. In his testimony Dr. Holtrop said that on the basis of her last menstrual period she would have been seventeen weeks pregnant at the time he saw her on September 21; but after examining her, he testified, he felt she was one month off—that she had either forgotten the date of her last menstrual period or misinterpreted minor spotting as if it were a period—and was actually about twenty-one weeks pregnant.

Actually, if Alice Roe were correct about the date of her last menstrual period, she would have been only thirteen weeks pregnant on September 21. Strangely, neither the prosecution nor the defense ever called attention to this error in Dr. Holtrop's calculations. In fact she must have been two months off on her dates; in order to be about twenty-one weeks pregnant on September 21, her last menstrual period would have begun on March 28, not May 28. The closest they came to making this apparent was in this exchange between Newman Flanagan and Dr. Holtrop during direct examination on Monday, January 13, 1975, the sixth day of the trial.

Question (by Flanagan): Doctor, if I told you that the record at the hospital indicates that "LMP [last menstrual period] May 28, 1973," would that help you at all as to

112

recalling when she told you her last menstrual period was?

Answer (by Holtrop): I cannot verify whether that was what she told me or not. I don't recall it in that sense.

I recall it in the sense that when she gave me a date I consulted a calendar, and calculated it as being seventeen weeks from the time of the first examination, eighteen weeks from the time of hospital admission.

At any rate this mathematical inconsistency was not of great consequence (I call attention to it only because I was surprised that neither attorney had done so), since all the doctors who examined Alice Roe concluded that her pregnancy was more advanced than the date, or dates, she gave them would suggest.

And here we arrive at the first of several serious discrepancies in the testimony of the physicians involved, either as participants or expert witnesses, in this case—the age of the fetus. Once the date of Alice Roe's last menstrual period was disregarded as unreliable, as it was by all the doctors who testified, then the only other method of determining the age of the fetus was by physical examination. (Actually, ultrasound, a procedure in which sound waves are used to determine the size of the fetal skull, could have been used. But in 1973 at Boston City Hospital the equipment had only recently been acquired, and the technician who worked with it did not have enough experience to give any more accurate estimations of the duration of pregnancy than could be derived from physical examination.)

There are two ways to estimate fetal age by physical examination. One is to use a tape measure to measure the distance between the symphysis pubis (the bony prominence at the lower end of the abdomen where the two sides of the pelvis meet) and the fundus, the top, of the uterus. The other is to simply use one's fingers to measure from the umbilicus to the

113

top of the uterus. Ordinarily in a pregnant woman the distance between the symphysis pubis and the umbilicus is twenty centimeters and the fundus reaches this point when the woman is twenty weeks pregnant. Then, as previously indicated, the fundus rises one fingerbreadth (approximately two centimeters) in each successive week. On October 1, the day after Alice Roe was admitted to the hospital, Dr. Holtrop used a tape measure and found that the distance between the symphysis and the top of her uterus was twenty-two centimeters. He therefore concluded that the fetus was about twenty-one weeks old.

When Dr. Giminez examined Alice Roe on September 30, he used his fingers to measure from the umbilicus to the top of the uterus and found the distance to be four fingerbreadths, or seven centimeters. He therefore estimated the fetal age at about twenty-four weeks. Alan Silberman, a medical student, examined Alice Roe just before and in the same way as did Dr. Gimenez, and he too had concluded that she was twenty-four weeks pregnant. (Silberman realized that his inexperience made his opinion of doubtful value and so wrote it on a corner of the chart to make certain it would not be given undue consideration.) Dr. Edelin, when he examined Alice Roe on October 2, just before attempting a saline abortion, used his fingers to measure the height of the uterus above the umbilicus and concluded she was between twenty and twenty-two weeks pregnant.

Why the discrepancy, and which doctors' estimates were most apt to be accurate? Dr. Holtrop pointed out in his testimony that though the distance between the symphysis and the umbilicus is usually about twenty centimeters in a pregnant woman, that distance may vary by as much as two or three centimeters. Therefore, he felt that a more reliable measurement is obtained by using a tape measure. There is no doubt that on this point Dr. Holtrop was correct.

It is also true that the height of the uterus may be affected by among other things, the urinary bladder. The urinary blad-

der lies just behind the symphysis and if it is full of urine it will displace the uterus upward. There was no record as to whether Alice Roe had emptied her bladder before the examination by Dr. Giminez or Alan Silberman; nor, as Dr. Holtrop admitted, was there any record as to whether or not her bladder was empty when he made his measurement. However, when Dr. Edelin examined Alice Roe on October 2, it is certain that the bladder was empty; the bladder is always emptied (by inserting a hollow rubber tube, a catheter) before an attempt is made to put a needle into the uterus. Otherwise it is possible, even probable, that the needle might perforate the bladder.

Greenhill's textbook on obstetrics (thirteenth edition) says, "The size of the uterus or the height of the fundus from the pubis or umbilicus is usually a valueless measurement, since so many conditions may alter it; for example, the amount of fat in the abdominal wall, tumors and gas in the abdomen, a full bladder or rectum, hydramnios [excessive amniotic fluid], twins, pendulous [flabby] abdomen and contracted pelvis." Greenhill also states, "Methods of determining the duration of pregnancy cannot be accurate because of inconstancy of the location of the umbilicus, thickness of the abdominal wall, the amount of amniotic fluid, the size of the fetus and the possibility of multiple pregnancy. Nevertheless an attempt should always be made to estimate its duration. At times the estimates will be fairly accurate." (p. 165)

Taking all these caveats into consideration, and realizing that not only did Dr. Holtrop and Dr. Edelin have more experience than Dr. Giminez or Mr. Silberman but that Dr. Holtrop used a tape measure and Dr. Edelin knew Alice Roe's bladder was empty at the time of his measurement, I think it can be safely concluded that Holtrop's and Edelin's estimates of fetal age at approximately twenty-one weeks were more likely to be accurate than Giminez' and Silberman's estimates of twenty-four weeks.

11

When Alice Roe was admitted to the hospital on September 30, Dr. Giminez listened to her abdomen with a fetoscope—a stethoscope specially designed for listening to the fetal heartbeat—and he recorded the rate at 140 beats a minute. This was within the normal range for a fetus anywhere between twenty and thirty-eight weeks of age. If any of the other doctors listened to the fetal heart tones, they did not note it on Alice Roe's chart, nor did they ever testify to it. In fact, all the doctors involved in the attempted saline abortions and in the eventual abortion by hysterotomy considered the presence or absence of a heartbeat to be irrelevant, since they intended to abort the fetus. Here, for example, is an exchange between Newman Flanagan and Dr. Holtrop.

Q. Now, Doctor, were you aware when you made your particular estimate of period of gestation that there was a fetal heartbeat of 140?

A. Am I aware that the rate was 140?

117

William A. Nolen, M.D.

Q. Yes.

A. No. I paid no attention to the rate of the fetal heart at the time of any examination that I did, I'm sorry.

Both Alice Roe (whose age is sometimes given as seventeen, at other times as eighteen) and her mother gave permission for the aminoglutethamide study that was done on October 1. There were some questions raised about proper authorization, but no one seriously questioned Alice Roe's willingness to cooperate. The study, which required the intravenous administration of aminoglutethamide followed by repeated sampling of the patient's blood, was completed on the morning of October 2. The study had been done in the patient's room, but now that it had been completed, she was taken to the room where saline infusions were done. And, as Dr. Edelin readily admitted, he attempted to carry out a saline infusion—or a "salting out," as the procedure is known.

This seems a practical point at which to discuss abortion techniques as they were generally practiced in October of 1973.

Up to about the twelfth week of pregnancy it was customary to use either a D & C (a dilatation and curettage) or a suction curettage to empty the uterus. In both techniques the first step is to stretch the opening at the lower end—the cervix—of the uterus. Then, if a curettage is to be performed, a sharp, spoonlike instrument (a curette) is inserted into the uterus and the inner lining of the uterus is scraped off and with it the fetus. All the scrapings flow into the vagina and are then mopped out and emptied into a basin or a similar receptacle. In a suction curettage a plastic tube is inserted into the uterus and aspiration, much like a vacuuming, is done, sucking the uterine contents into a jar. In very early pregnancies the suction curettage can be done without a general anesthetic; sedation with a tranquilizer and possibly some painkilling

118

medication is all that is necessary. For more advanced pregnancies and for those in which curettage with a metal curette is used, general anesthesia is usually necessary.

After twelve weeks the fetus is usually too large to be successfully removed either by dilatation and curettage or by suction. So, for pregnancies beyond the twelfth week, either saline abortion or hysterotomy is performed. In a saline abortion, as we've noted, a needle is inserted into the amniotic sac and a concentrated salt solution is injected after removing some of the amniotic fluid. Anywhere from eight to seventy-two hours after the injection of the salt solution, the patient goes into labor and the fetus is expelled.

No one knows with certainty why the injection of a concentrated salt solution causes the patient to abort. Possibly it burns or scalds the fetus so that the fetus dies and, as almost invariably happens (probably due to hormonal changes), once the fetus is dead the uterus contracts and expels it. However, since occasionally saline abortion results in the expulsion of a live fetus, this explanation is not always adequate. Another theory—that the solution stimulates the uterus so that it contracts and expels the fetus—may explain some, if not all, saline abortions.

Between the twelfth and sixteenth week it may be difficult to get a needle into the amniotic sac, since it is relatively small and there is not much fluid around the fetus. If this is the case, then the amniocentesis and salting out cannot be safely done. Sometimes, as in the Alice Roe case, even when the fetus is older than sixteen weeks, mechanical problems, in particular a placenta which is attached to the inner front wall of the uterus, may make it impossible for the doctor to get the needle into the amniotic sac. The doctor knows his needle is in the sac when he is able to draw back clear amniotic fluid. If he withdraws blood, then he knows he is not in the amniotic sac and so cannot proceed with the injection of saline.

119

Here is Edelin's testimony as to what happened during the attempts at saline abortion. Homans is the questioner, the answers are Edelin's.

Q. What did you do then [after the bloody taps] so far as this particular patient was concerned?

A. I explained to the patient the difficulty I was having and the reasons why I could not proceed with the injection of the saline and the possible hazards that it would have to her.

At some point that afternoon, and I don't remember exactly when, I went to seek consultation with Dr. Penza, because he had more experience in saline infusion than I had.

Q. By the way, what was Dr. Penza's position at Boston City Hospital and what was your position?

A. At that time?

Q. Yes.

A. I was chief resident, and Dr. Penza was either associate or assistant director. I think he was associate director of the department.

Q. And what took place at this consultation, sir?

A. I asked him if he would attempt to perform the saline abortion for me because I was having difficulty getting into the amniotic cavity. He indicated to me that he would attempt to perform the saline the next day in the operating room, and if that failed, a hysterotomy should be done.

Q. Sir, at about what time of day was this?

A. It was sometime in the afternoon of October 2.

Dr. Edelin put Alice Roe on the operating schedule for the next morning, so that the nurses would have an operating room reserved and instruments prepared for an attempted saline and possible hysterotomy. Alice was then returned to her

120

room where she would, hopefully, recover from the stress of the unsuccessful attempts at saline abortion and get the rest that would prepare her for the hysterotomy.

After reading Dr. Hugh Holtrop's testimony, I thought it might be profitable to meet and talk with him. When I had phoned Dr. Holtrop from Minnesota to ask him to discuss his role in the Edelin case, he had been wary. "I just don't feel comfortable discussing that case—or any patient, for that matter—over the telephone with someone I've never met." I told him I would send him one of the books I had written, so that he could see, I hoped, that I wanted to get at the relevant truth in the case, that I wasn't interested in writing an exposé. I also told him I was willing to come to Boston and meet with him at his convenience. Under these conditions he agreed to see me.

We met at his office in Boston, near the Beth Israel Hospital, at 11:00 A.M. on February 2, 1977. He was dressed informally, wearing an open-necked, colorful sport shirt under his white coat, and he treated me very cordially and discussed the Edelin case freely, with the one understandable exception that he would not reveal anything about "Alice Roe" that might enable me to identify her.

Holtrop is husky, but not fat, about 6 feet tall. He looks as if he might have played football, probably as a blocking back, in college. He has a ruddy complexion and a face that struck me as "square," in the geometric sense. He was born in 1931, so in 1973, at the time of the Edelin case, he was forty-two years old. He was then chief of the obstetrical-gynecological outpatient department at Boston City Hospital, a part-time job. He gave up that position in 1974 when Ed Lowe became full-time chief of obstetrics at Boston City.

"Dr. Lowe and I had some fundamental philosophical disagreements," Holtrop told me. "I'm very interested in family planning. I felt very strongly that we needed an active adoles-

121

cent gynecology clinic at Boston City Hospital, a place where young people could get information and counseling not only about abortion but about contraception and venereal disease. I felt that sort of center deserved top priority if we were ever going to get at the roots of the abortion problem. We needed to prevent unwanted pregnancies. Lowe disagreed. He was interested in fancy endocrinology and bizarre tumors. As far as unwanted pregnancies were concerned he seemed to think that our mission was not prevention but treatment. I couldn't get his support for the adolescent gynecology clinic, so I left.

"Besides," he added, "with my children reaching the age where they needed—at least in my opinion—private education, I had to devote more time to earning a living, and that meant added concentration on private practice; though if I could have gotten the support I wanted at Boston City Hospital, I would have stuck with that job."

As far as the role he played in the Edelin case, here is Holtrop's story as he told it to me. I realize that I have covered some of this material earlier, but it seems worth emphasizing.

"It was late in the afternoon of September 23 when this young girl and her mother arrived at the outpatient department. I was the only doctor still there. Even the counselors had left. She told me her story and I examined her. According to the menstrual history she gave me, she should have been seventeen weeks pregnant, but from the size of her uterus, I estimated she was a month off and about twenty weeks pregnant. I spent a lot of time counseling her—advising her of all the alternatives to abortion open to her—and then, because of her particular circumstances, which I am not going to tell you about, I agreed that abortion was the proper choice for her. I arranged for her to be admitted a week or so later, and since I was the only doctor still in the outpatient department, I signed the admission sheet. She was not in any sense one of my private patients. I hadn't ever met the girl till that afternoon."

(Edelin, in his trial testimony, claimed he was casually in-

122

troduced to Alice Roe at the time of this initial visit to Boston City Hospital. But Edelin did not examine or counsel her at that time.)

"The next time I saw Alice Roe was on October 1, after she had been admitted to the hospital. As I testified, I looked at the chart, noted that Giminez and the medical student thought she was twenty-four weeks pregnant, but I still felt certain she was less than twenty-two weeks pregnant; though, to be perfectly honest, I think in her case I would have recommended abortion even if she were twenty-five weeks pregnant. For her, in my opinion, an abortion was an absolute necessity.

"As you know, I was then doing a study on aminoglutethamide and both Alice Roe and her mother agreed to participate. The study took one day and was completed by the morning of October 2. As far as Alice Roe was concerned, my connection with her case ended after that study was performed. At that time Ken Edelin, Dr. Charles and whatever other doctors were involved in the actual performance of abortions in the hospital took responsibility for her case. My duties at Boston City were limited to the outpatient department."

It was now about noon, and Dr. Holtrop asked one of his aides if she'd mind picking us up a couple of pastrami sandwiches and some pickles at a nearby delicatessen. "We can talk a bit more while we eat, if you like," he said. "I'm free for another hour."

I thanked him and then asked how he felt about the case against Edelin. "Personally," he said, "I think Ken was shabbily treated. It seemed to me that Charles and Penza and the others who were involved in the abortion could and should have given him more support. I also think that Ken should never have testified before the grand jury. My lawyer advised me not to answer any questions in regard to the Alice Roe case, and I'm surprised that Ken's lawyer didn't give him the same advice. Of course after the indictment he retained a different lawyer—Homans—who is reportedly excellent.

123

William A. Nolen, M.D.

"My lawyer did offer to have me meet informally with Newman Flanagan, but Flanagan said no to that. He wanted to talk to me in the presence of the grand jury or not at all.

"Let me make another thing clear," Holtrop said. "I am not proabortion. I think abortions are the worst of all methods of birth control. I find abortions—particularly after the first trimester—absolutely repulsive. I feel strongly that abortion after the first trimester should only be performed for the most compelling reasons—medical, social or psychological. Abortion is both an evil and a social necessity. It's a dehumanizing answer but one we occasionally must accept. I hate abortions, but I do them."

Hugh Holtrop struck me as a dedicated physician, ambivalent about his role as an occasional abortionist, and a very compassionate man.

12

When he questioned Dr. Holtrop, Bill Homans wanted to get to the jurors the message that the failed attempts at saline abortion might actually have killed the fetus in Alice Roe's uterus. If the fetus had died on October 2 as a result of the bloody taps, then, of course, Dr. Edelin could not possibly have committed manslaughter on the fetus when he did the hysterotomy on October 3.

Newman Flanagan felt there was no evidence to suggest that the taps had killed the fetus and that it would be improper for the jury to listen to any questioning that might lead them to such a false conclusion. The judge decided to listen to Homans and Flanagan argue their respective positions out of the hearing of the jury, so he held a *voir dire* meeting. In a *voir dire* only the judge, the lawyers, the court reporters and the witness, if necessary, are present. It is a meeting in which the judge listens to the questions that will be asked and to the responses of the witness and then decides whether or not his

testimony ought to be heard by the jurors. Here are excerpts from the *voir dire* meeting with Dr. Holtrop:

The Court: Mr. Foreman and ladies and gentlemen of the jury: We have a problem concerning evidence. I'm going to hear it in the absence of the jury. It will take some time. You are excused until tomorrow morning at ten o'clock.
(The jury thereupon filed out of the courtroom.)
The Court: Now, counsel, on this projected line of inquiry I will hear you on *voir dire.*
Mr. Homans: Yes, your Honor.
Voir dire by Mr. Homans
Q. Dr. Holtrop, coming back to the quote "bloody taps" end of quote to which you referred, as I understand your testimony, those bloody taps will occur as a result of the insertion of the needle somewhere in the uterus without going into the amniotic fluid, is that correct?
A. They may, yes.
Q. And will you please correct me if I am wrong on terminology or order or anything like that. Now, a bloody tap may arise, may it not, either from insertion into a placental blood vessel, from insertion into a portion of the fetus, or from what other cause that you are aware of, in your opinion?
A. Insertion into a maternal blood vessel.
Q. Or insertion into a maternal blood vessel. So those are the three possibilities?
A. Yes.
Q. And whether or not a bloody tap could occur as a result of any other location of the needle when amniocentesis is being performed?
A. I think that covers all the possibilities.
Q. And if any one of those three possibilities did not oc-

126

cur, whether or not in your opinion there would have been a bloody tap?

A. There would not have been.

Q. Because then the needle would have gone where?

A. It would have been in the amniotic cavity if clear fluid had been obtained.

Q. Now, did you have an opinion as to the effect on the placenta if the needle goes into a placental blood vessel?

A. Yes, I have an opinion.

Q. What is that opinion?

A. I wish that I could qualify it with facts. My opinion is that it carries a risk of hemorrhage from the placenta itself, and thereby implies a risk of anemia on the part of the fetus. But unfortunately, that's an opinion and I don't have facts at my disposal to tell you how often it happens.

Q. Well, do you have an opinion, with that qualification, or with or without that qualification, as to the effect of the needle going into a portion of the fetus?

A. I think that the same thing is quite possible, and it carries with it a significant hazard. But I can't quantify it for you.

Q. And so far as going into a maternal blood vessel is concerned, whether or not it is less likely or more likely that this would cause some damage to the fetus?

A. The maternal blood vessel would be unlikely to cause damage to the fetus. But it is the hazard in doing this procedure in which we find the—well, what we consider the worst of the possibilities.

Q. And whether or not in your opinion, insofar as the needle being inserted into a placental blood vessel, or the needle being inserted into a portion of the fetus, whether or not you have an opinion as to whether or

127

not that would create a significant risk of termination of the existence of the fetus, either of those two?

A. I think that would carry with it a risk of termination of the fetal existence, but whether it's significant or not, I cannot quantify it. I do not know.

Mr. Homans: That would be the extent of my questioning of this witness, your Honor. May I have a moment, your Honor?

(Mr. Homans conferring with client and co-counsel.)

Q. One more question. Given damage to a placental blood vessel causing hemorrhage, whether or not you have an opinion as to whether that could cause anoxia to the fetus, yes or no?

A. Yes, it can.

Mr. Homans: I have no further questions.

Voir dire by Mr. Flanagan

Q. So that, Doctor, what you say is, it's possible that the needle could go into the placenta, and that that injection of the needle into the placenta could cause anoxia to the fetus?

A. Yes, it could.

Q. To what extent?

A. Depending upon how much hemorrhage resulted, depending upon whether any hemorrhage resulted, depending upon whether infection resulted. This is a theoretical question.

The judge considered the matter overnight, asked Dr. Holtrop a few additional questions during a *voir dire* the next morning and then decided that his testimony on the consequences of bloody tap was too speculative to be heard or considered by the jury.

One fact is certain—according to the record, at no time after Dr. Giminez listened to the fetal heart on September 30 did

128

anyone make any attempt to find out whether the fetus was still living—something that could have been determined in ten seconds if anyone had had the desire or felt there was any need to do so.

On the morning of October 3, as mentioned previously, Dr. Penza tried, in the operating room under local anesthesia, to perform a saline abortion. His results were, as Dr. Edelin's had been, unsuccessful; he got a bloody tap. After explaining to Alice Roe that the tap had again been unsuccessful, an anesthetist was called and she was given a general anesthesia. As the nurses washed the patient's abdomen with a sterlizing solution and applied the appropriate drapes, Dr. Edelin went out into the corridor, found Steven Teich to act as an assistant, and scrubbed his hands in preparation for performing the hysterotomy. Edelin testified that it took him five minutes to find Teich and another ten minutes to scrub. Prosecution and the defense agreed that this was, indeed, the sequence of events.

However, as a surgeon with twenty-four years of experience (if my internship and residency are included, as they should be) I can suggest at least one question that I think should have been asked at this point in the trial. If Dr. Edelin expected that he would have to do a hysterotomy that morning—and after his experience with several unsuccessful taps the previous day he must have known a hysterotomy was almost inevitable—why hadn't he arranged on October 2 to have a capable assistant available on the morning of October 3? Particularly when, according to Edelin's testimony (19-122), he had, prior to October 3, 1973, never personally done a hysterotomy for abortion and had only been involved in about twelve. Nor had he ever been involved in a case where the hysterotomy for abortion was being done on a patient who was somewhere around twenty-two to twenty-four weeks pregnant. The hysterotomy he was about to perform was different from any with which he had ever before even

129

been associated as an assistant, let alone as a surgeon, and yet he had made no arrangements to have an experienced assistant help him. As a surgeon who spent five years at Bellevue acquiring the skills needed to do my job, I consider Edelin's nonchalance difficult to understand.

No matter, whatever the reason, on October 3, with a third-year medical student assisting him, Edelin embarked on his first attempt to perform a hysterotomy on a woman who was approximately twenty-two weeks pregnant.

Now we come to a very critical point in the Edelin case; the actual performance of the hysterotomy. Crucial to the operation was Edelin's attitude to the patient and the fetus in her uterus. Here is what Edelin had to say about his obligations to each (questions by Flanagan, answers by Edelin, 20-78).

> **Q.** Doctor, in an abortion do you consider whether you owe any duty to the fetus?
>
> **A.** Not at the outset, no.
>
> **Q.** So that your only duty at the outset is concerning the mother?
>
> **A.** Yes, sir.
>
> **Q.** So that just prior to the commencement of your hysterotomy in this case you felt you had no duty to the fetus, is that correct?
>
> **A.** That's correct.
>
> **Q.** And you also felt that whether the fetus was alive was not important, is that correct?
>
> **A.** At the start of the hysterotomy?
>
> **Q.** Prior to the commencement of this specific hysterotomy?
>
> **A.** Yes, sir.
>
> **Q.** And therefore, Doctor, your only concern at that time was with the mother?
>
> **A.** Yes, sir.

* * *

Another exchange between Flanagan and Edelin helps elucidate Edelin's attitude toward Alice Roe and her fetus (20-38). Questions, again, by Flanagan; answers by Edelin.

Q. And as a matter of fact you weren't sure if this particular subject was alive or dead at that time.

Mr. Homans: At what time?

Mr. Flanagan : At the commencement of the hysterotomy.

The Court: Don't answer.

Mr. Homans: I withdraw the objection.

The Court: Now you may answer.

A. That's correct.

Q. And it would have made no difference to you?

A. No, sir.

Q. Well, let me ask you this, Doctor: Assume that the fetus was alive. Would you have a pediatrician there in the O.R. with you?

A. No.

Q. Why?

A. Because this was an abortion.

Q. So what does that mean to you, Doctor?

A. This was an abortion being performed before viability, and I thought that would be, No. 1, contrary to the patient's wishes, and contrary to good medical practice.

In fairness to Dr. Edelin I must also make it clear that: (1) he did not believe that Alice Roe's fetus was viable, i.e., capable of living outside the uterus; (2) in the remote possibility that the abortion resulted in a living fetus, he claimed he would have immediately sent it to the intensive care unit for the newborn.

Now we come to the hysterotomy itself. There was more testimony and argument over this procedure and the circum-

131

stances that surrounded it than over any other aspect of the case. Expert witnesses testified both in support of and against Edelin's performance of the operation. Whether one approved and condoned his behavior or criticized and condemned it depended to a large extent on one's experience and personal prejudices. In the matter of the clocks—which we shall come to soon—confusion reigned supreme, and those who either read or heard the testimony could honestly reach divergent conclusions. I shall try to summarize all the data as objectively, completely and honestly as I can.

First, it should be made clear that a hysterotomy is—as far as operations are concerned—a rather simple procedure, far easier to perform, in most cases, than an appendectomy or a tonsillectomy. "Hysterotomy" means, literally, "to open the uterus," just as "thoracotomy" means "to open the thorax" (thorax means chest) or "phlebotomy" means "to open a vein" (phlebos means vein). When a surgeon does a hysterotomy for the purpose of abortion, what he is actually doing is opening the uterus and removing the products of conception.

The differences between a hysterotomy for abortion and a Caesarian section are (1) that the goal of a Caesarian section is to remove a baby capable of living outside its mother's uterus, while that of a hysterotomy for abortion is to remove a fetus before it reaches the age of viability and (2) when the hysterotomy for abortion, or mini-Caesarean section, is done, the pregnancy is generally not as far advanced as it is at the time of a Caesarean section, so the uterus and the products of conception are proportionately smaller.

Although I am a general surgeon, not a specialist in obstetrics and gynecology, I have, over the last seventeen years, performed many Caesarean sections. When I do the hysterotomy that is part of every Caesarean section, my goal is always to obtain a live baby. Sometimes I have to get the operation done very quickly. If I am doing the Caesarean section

because the mother has started to bleed massively because her placenta is attached to the uterus over its cervix (a so-called *placenta praevia*) or because a slowing down of the fetal heart rate suggests that the fetus is in distress (perhaps because of a twisted umbilical cord), I want to get that baby out as rapidly as possible so that we can give it whatever help it may need to survive.

This does not mean that I would operate in such a fashion that I would jeopardize the mother's life, or even add minimally to the risk to her life, in order to save the baby. Nor can I conceive of any situation where I would have to make such a choice. It is very simple to do the Caesarean section—or hysterotomy—quickly, in the best interest of the baby, without increasing in any way the risk to the mother.

When the baby is in jeopardy, it ought to be possible to have the baby out and in the hands of the pediatrician, nurse or anesthetist who will work to keep it alive within five minutes of the time the mother has been anesthetized. All the surgeon must do is cut through the abdominal wall (a vertical incision through the midline of the lower abdomen should take less than a minute), make an incision into the uterus (either a vertical or horizontal incision can be used, but the vertical can be made most quickly; in either case one minute is more than enough time to make the hysterotomy incision) and open the amniotic sac (at which point amniotic fluid will spurt out of the uterus, in my experience almost invariably soaking right through my scrub suit and undershorts). Opening the amniotic sac takes about two seconds; the only care that must be exercised is not to nick the baby who may be floating just beneath the thin membrane. Then the surgeon reaches into the uterus, grabs the baby by a foot or its head, whichever is most easily located, and pulls the child through the hole in the uterus. This may take another minute—at most, two. Then the operator puts two clamps across the umbilical cord near its center (five seconds), cuts between them, detaching the child from

133

the placenta, and hands the baby to the nurse or doctor, who will suck mucus out of its mouth, blow air or oxygen into its lungs or do anything else that may be necessary to make the baby cry; crying is good for the newborn infant, since it helps to expand the lungs.

While others are working with the baby, the surgeon peels the amniotic sac and the placenta from the inside of the uterus, injects drugs into the uterus to make its muscular wall contract (which helps stop uterine bleeding) and then closes the opening in the uterus—the hysterotomy—with two or three layers of sutures. After mopping out any amniotic fluid or blood that may have spilled into the abdomen, he closes the abdominal wall. Since the uterus is now much smaller than it was before the removal of the baby, the abdominal wall is usually relaxed and can be quickly and easily closed. An experienced surgeon can perform an uncomplicated Caesarean section, from incision to completed closure ("skin to skin," as they say in the surgery business) in half an hour, forty-five minutes at most.

Now, however, we must consider a hysterotomy done for abortion, as was the case where Dr. Edelin and Alice Roe were concerned. Based on my interpretation of the testimony—and I think the testimony is very clear—here is what I consider a fair and honest summary of what went on during the hysterotomy phase of the case.

In this situation there was no need to hurry. Not only did no one know whether the fetus was in distress, no one cared. (In fact, in Alice Roe's case, no one had even bothered to determine whether the fetus was alive or dead.) There was no reason to hurry to save the fetus' life. In fact, the opposite was true; if the fetus was alive when the hysterotomy for abortion began, it was probably best to go slow, in the hope that the prolonged administration of anesthesia (some of which passes through the placenta to the fetus) might kill the fetus by the time the surgeon was ready to remove it from the uterus. Af-

134

ter all, the goal of a hysterotomy for abortion is a dead fetus, not a live one. (I failed to mention that one of the indications for haste when performing a Caesarean section, particularly when the baby's life is in danger, is to keep the infant's exposure to anesthesia to a minimum. With the newer anesthetics this is not as necessary as it once was, but in critical cases it may still be an important factor.)

The first evidence that Edelin was not concerned about the well-being of the fetus—other than his own admission of the fact—was his choice of an abdominal incision. Instead of the vertical incision in the lower midline of the abdomen, an incision that goes through a relatively bloodless part of the abdominal wall and can be made speedily, Edelin chose to use a Pfannenstiel incision. A Pfannenstiel incision, named after the surgeon who devised it, is a slightly curved but almost transverse incision that is made just at the top of or very slightly above the pubic hair line; the pubic hair is shaved off before any lower abdominal incision. The Pfannenstiel incision has, since the bikini was designed, been known as the bikini incision, because it is low enough to be covered by the top of a bikini bathing suit.

It takes longer to make a Pfannenstiel incision than it does to make a vertical incision. The extra time is necessary because, once the transverse incision is made through the skin and fat, the skin and fat at the top of the incision must be peeled back so that the underlying muscles can be split vertically to expose the peritoneum. A few more vessels are cut in the subcutaneous fat as the incision is made, and these must be clamped and tied. It also takes a few extra minutes to peel back the upper flap of skin and fat in order to get proper exposure of the underlying muscles, so that the opening into the abdomen will be large enough to permit the surgeon to insert his whole hand and bring forth the contents of the uterus. Some surgeons feel that a Pfannenstiel incision is stronger than a vertical midline incision, but its main advantage is cos-

metic. Once it has healed, the scar can hardly be seen because of the pubic hair.

An experienced surgeon might need five or ten minutes to make a Pfannenstiel incision (as opposed to one or two minutes for a midline incision), but in the Alice Roe case Edelin testified it took him twenty to thirty minutes to make the incision. He attributed this, in part, to the inexperience of his assistant (the third-year medical student, whom Edelin had asked to assist) and also in part to the fact that Edelin "was also teaching him as we went along." Edelin, by his own testimony, implicitly admitted that he was in no particular hurry to reach this fetus.

Once Edelin had reached the uterus, he elected to make a low transverse incision in the uterus. Again, this takes more time than the vertical incision most surgeons would use to quickly get to a fetus in distress. The bladder must be peeled off the uterus before this incision can be made, and care must be taken not to cut too widely and that the uterus doesn't tear as the contents are removed, for fear the large uterine arteries that run along the sides of the uterus will also be torn, resulting in heavy and potentially dangerous bleeding. The advantage to a transverse incision in the uterus is that it is generally considered stronger than a vertical incision and is less apt to rupture if the patient becomes pregnant later. (Spontaneous uterine rupture through any incision is rare. In the seventeen years I have practiced in Litchfield, we have never had a spontaneous rupture of a previous uterine incision, even though every doctor on our staff uses vertical incisions when doing Caesarean sections.)

When Edelin had finally incised the uterine muscle (an incision about three fingerbreadths in length) and had reached the amniotic sac, he testified that he then inserted two fingers into the uterine opening and tried to separate the placenta and the amniotic sac from the inner wall of the uterus without rupturing the amniotic sac. His purpose in doing this, he said, was to

prevent infection or hemorrhage from developing later, which might be the case if any of the products of conception were left behind, attached to the uterine wall. He referred to textbooks that recommended this particular technique be used in performing abortion by hysterotomy.

Unfortunately, what he did not point out—but what was pointed out by witnesses for the prosecution—was that this particular technique, in which all the products of conception are removed intact, is feasible only up until the sixteenth week. After the sixteenth week, the products of conception are usually too large to be removed intact through the standard uterine incision. And, as Dr. William O'Connell, a prosecution witness, testified, in his opinion to remove intact a fetus, placenta and amniotic sac the size of those in Alice Roe's uterus would be "a surgical impossibility."

I am not suggesting that Dr. Edelin knew that what he was attempting to do was a surgical impossibility. He admittedly had never attempted abortion by hysterotomy in a pregnancy as advanced as Alice Roe's. Dr. Ed Lowe, who later became chief of obstetrics at Boston City Hospital told me when I asked him about Dr. Edelin's venture, "Ken had never done an abortion in a case like this one. I think he just read the books and thought, 'If it can be done at sixteen weeks, it can probably be done at twenty-two'—or however pregnant the patient was. Obviously, he was wrong."

In fairness to Dr. Edelin I concede that it is possible he simply made an error in judgment, an error of the sort surgeons in training not infrequently make.

Even though he had never done a hysterotomy for abortion, Edelin may have thought, having done other hysterotomies, that a hysterotomy for abortion would be a relatively simply operation. Hysterotomy, remember, only means "open the uterus," a procedure he had done whenever he performed a Caesarian section. After reading about how to perform hysterotomy abortions he may have felt that he would not need

expert or experienced help in operating on Alice Roe. I think he was surprised, when he finally reached and cut into the uterus, at how thick the muscle of the uterus was at this stage of pregnancy and how richly supplied with blood vessels it was. I think it wasn't till he actually began to open the uterus that he realized this hysterotomy for abortion was going to be much more difficult to perform than he had anticipated. He had, I think, been misled by how simple the operation sounded when he read about it in a surgical textbook.

Having been a surgical resident, and having fallen into this sort of trap myself (with other operations; I've never done an abortion of any kind), I can sympathize with Dr. Edelin. The authors who write textbooks on surgical technique are always experts and they often make operations sound easier to perform than, for those less experienced, they are. (I am sorry that, in this book, I continually have to guess at what Edelin's experiences and feelings were. However, since he absolutely refused to discuss the case with me, I have no other choice than to reach whatever conclusions seem to me reasonable, based on Edelin's testimony, other interviews he gave, and my own experience as a surgeon.)

In any event, in answer to a question by Bill Homans, Dr. Edelin testified to his next steps in the abortion once he had entered the uterus. (19-84):

A. Then I inserted my fingers, two fingers into the incision, and attempted to sweep around the inside to separate the placenta and the amniotic sac from the inside of the uterus. After doing that, I attempted to ease the products of conception, that is, the amniotic sac and the placenta attached to it and the fetus within it, out of the incision.
Q. With how many hands?
A. I was using my left hand.
Q. Yes, sir. What did you do with your right hand, sir?

138

A. I used it to steady the uterus.

Q. And when you described the process a moment ago about sweeping your fingers around, was that with your left hand or with your right hand, sir?

A. That was with my left hand.

Q. Now, you say you attempted to ease the products of conception out. How did you do that, sir?

A. By putting my two fingers into the incision behind the sac and trying to ease it out of the incision, but unfortunately the sac broke.

Q. And how long would you say the sac broke after the time when you first got into the uterus, after you first put your fingers into the uterus, sir?

A. From the first time?

Q. From the time you first put your finger in the uterus as you described and separated or ran your finger around inside the uterus?

A. It doesn't take an extremely long time to separate the placenta and the amniotic sac from the uterine wall, I would say maybe fifteen or twenty seconds. Then I attempted to ease the products of conception out of the incision, and I would say that the rupture of the amniotic sac occurred very shortly thereafter.

Q. And what did you do when the amniotic sac ruptured, sir?

A. With my two fingers I attempted to grasp one of the lower extremities of the fetus to extract it from the uterus.

Q. Could you again show with the two fingers how you did that, sir?

(The witness demonstrates.)

Q. Then what happened, sir, and what did you do?

A. I attempted to extract the fetus from the uterus. Unfortunately, I had some difficulty, and it was a difficult extraction.

139

Q. And tell us whether or not you eventually accomplished the extraction, sir, as well as the nature of the difficulty you had. Describe the difficulty you had first.

A. Well, the problem was that making the incision in the lower uterine segment, or the area of the lower portion of the uterus, a very thick muscle, that it doesn't give. And the incision was small. That is because that portion of the uterus is small and narrow. It was difficult getting the fingers out of that incision.

Q. And whether or not you eventually got the fetus out of the incision?

A. Yes, sir.

Q. And what did you do then, sir?

A. After the fetus was removed, I observed it, and in the process of passing it from the operative field to a stainless steel basin, which my scrub tech was handing me, I also checked it for a heartbeat by touching the anterior chest wall.

Q. By doing what?

A. By touching the anterior chest wall.

Q. And whether or not you were looking for a sign of life, is that correct, sir?

A. Yes, sir.

Q. And what else did you do after you had examined by touching the chest, sir?

A. I placed the fetus in the stainless steel container that the operating room tech had handed me.

Q. And what did you do then?

A. I turned my attention back to the patient and I removed the rest of the placenta, took a sponge, wiped out the inside of the uterus to remove any remaining membranes, because the membranes had ruptured, from the uterine cavity. Took an instrument, passed it down through the cervix from the inside to open up

the cervix so it would have proper drainage and proceeded to repair the incision in the uterus.

Q. Now, how long, sir, would you say you took from the time that the fetus was delivered from the uterus to the instant when you passed the fetus to the scrub tech, sir?

A. From here to here, a couple of seconds.

Q. And it was during that period that you felt for a heartbeat, was it, sir?

A. Yes, sir.

Q. And can you give us, sir, then your best recollection of the time it took you from the point when you completed the incision into the uterus and put your finger inside the uterus to the time when you removed the fetus just before you handed it to the scrub tech, sir?

A. It probably took a couple of minutes.

Q. Was there any time, sir, when you looked at the clock in the operating room while holding your finger or hand in the uterus for a prolonged period of time, sir?

A. Absolutely not.

13

We now come to a matter which was disputed tediously and at great length during Dr. Edelin's trial. Did he or did he not, after detaching the placenta from the uterine wall, stand with his hand in the uterus and watch the clock for three or four minutes before he delivered the fetus?

The obvious implication of a positive answer to this question is that Dr. Edelin, having discovered that—despite his leisurely surgical approach—the fetus in Alice Roe's uterus was alive, had then separated the placenta from the uterus, in effect, cutting the pipeline through which oxygen could reach the fetus, and had then waited for three or four minutes so that the fetus would be dead before he delivered it from the uterus.

Dr. Enrique Giminez was the only person who testified, both before the grand jury and during the trial, that Dr. Edelin purposely delayed delivery for these critical minutes, while staring at the clock on the wall. During both direct and cross

examination Giminez held firmly to his position, which was that Dr. Edelin, immediately after cutting into the uterus, made a sweeping motion with his hand, a motion like that used to separate the placenta from the uterus. Then, Giminez testified, "He left his hand in the uterus and looked at the clock." Flanagan went on with his questioning of Giminez:

Q. All right. What, if anything, did you observe in connection with his hand?
A. At the time he was looking at the clock—nothing.
Q. You observed nothing? Were you watching?
A. Yes.
Q. And where is the clock?
A. It was on the operating room wall.
Q. All right. How long did he look at the clock?
A. At least three minutes.
Q. And during that three-minute period were you observing Dr. Edelin?
A. Yes.
Q. What, if anything, did you observe him doing?
A. He was looking at the clock.
Q. How about—
A. Nothing else.
Q. Nothing else. Whether or not there was any movement that you observed concerning the defendant in this case?
A. No, he was still looking at the clock.
Q. It was still and he was looking at the clock. And you have told us that that was for approximately three minutes?
A. Yes, sir.

As has already been noted, Edelin denied he ever stopped all hand motion and stared at a clock for three minutes. But

Giminez was adamant. He testified repeatedly that this was, in fact, what Edelin had done.

Enrique Giminez did not testify against Edelin because he didn't like Edelin or was "out to get him"; Giminez testified because he had no other choice. And he told the truth, as he saw the truth, because he felt an obligation not to lie, and also, admittedly, because he had no desire to go to jail for perjury.

Giminez, who had been educated at the University of Mexico, was, at the time of the trial, the chief resident in obstetrics at Cambridge City Hospital, a hospital associated with Tufts Medical School (Cambridge is a suburb of Boston). I talked, in September of 1977, with an associate professor of obstetrics at Tufts who was on the staff of the Cambridge City Hospital and knew and worked closely with Giminez during his year as chief resident.

This doctor (whom I shall call "Dr. Smith," not his real name) told me, "Giminez was an excellent resident. He had good hands; he was a superb operator. He was smart, too, and he read a lot. He kept up with the obstetrical literature.

"Several times, while he was with us at Cambridge, I drove him into Boston when he had to testify at Edelin's trial. Naturally, we sometimes discussed the case.

"One thing you should understand is that when Giminez was called to testify before the grand jury, he had no idea that he was going to be questioned about Alice Roe. He thought he was going to be asked about the antibiotic experiments on fetuses—the "grave-robbers" case.

"Once he was before the grand jury he had no choice, or at least none that he could think of, except to answer the questions. He had nothing against Edelin; he considered Edelin a friend. He hated being put in a position where he might have

145

to say something that would hurt Ken. There was simply no alternative."*

"Why did he leave Boston City and go to Cambridge?" I asked Dr. Smith.

"Well, as you might imagine, once he had testified before the grand jury, there were people at Boston City Hospital who were vicious toward him. Not—I should emphasize—Edelin. Edelin knew the spot Giminez had been in and continued to treat him fairly, as a friend and junior co-worker.

"But Edelin was only the chief resident. One of the higher-ups in the obstetrical department got very nasty. For example, Giminez was scheduled to rotate through Framingham, which is associated with the obstetrical department at Boston University and is one of the choice rotations for a junior resident. This guy at Boston City took that rotation away from Giminez. It was one way to 'get even' with him for testifying.

"At that point Giminez could see that his future in the BU program at Boston City wasn't very bright. Giminez comes from a very well-to-do family in Mexico. His father is a successful obstetrician and is a professor of obstetrics at one of the universities in Mexico. He was willing to back his son, and Giminez went so far as to retain one of the big Yankee law firms to represent him; he was going to fight what he felt was unjustified treatment of him at Boston City.

"Then—and wisely, I suppose—he decided to drop it. Even if he won the case he'd have had to spend his year as chief

*I asked Newman Flanagan (on October 31, 1977) whether it was possible that Giminez might not have realized what case he was going to be questioned about. "Very possible," Newman said. "When we go to court to get subpoena powers we simply label the case, whatever it is, ' *Commonwealth* v. *John Doe* ' and that's what's on the subpoena. Since the newspapers at that time were full of the 'grave-robber' case, Giminez might easily have believed that was the one about which we wanted to question him. It may have been a complete surprise to him when we started asking him about Edelin."

resident working with doctors and nurses who resented him. Instead he made a few phone calls, talked to one of the professors at Tufts and came to Cambridge City."

"How did things go for him over there?" I asked.

"Professionally, no problem. As I've told you, he was a damn good doctor and an excellent resident. While the trial was going on, he did suffer some harassment. One of the Boston papers—you noticed, I suppose, that they were strongly pro-Edelin?—even stooped to sending a female reporter over here in the role of a patient so that she could interview him. When things got really hot, we sent him away for a couple of weeks of vacation. By the time he got back, things were all right again. In fact, I was with him once, after the trial, when we bumped into Edelin at a medical meeting. Edelin said something like 'Hi, Ricky, how's it going?' and Giminez told him 'Fine, how is it with you?' and they talked for a few minutes.

"Once, just before he finished his year as resident, one of the other junior doctors did say something nasty to him in front of some nurses—something about ratting on a fellow doctor. Giminez was not a big man, but he had guts. He grabbed this guy's stethoscope from around his neck, took it apart, and threw the pieces on the floor. Then he invited the loudmouth to step outside."

"Did the loudmouth go?" I asked.

"Of course not," Smith told me. "He had just been trying to act like a big man in front of the nurses, and Giminez had called his bluff."

"Where's Giminez now?" I asked.

"Back in Mexico, working with his father. He's an assistant professor of obstetrics at the University of Mexico and involved in research on premature infants. When he finished his residency at Cambridge, he was invited to join one of the best obstetrical groups in the area at an excellent starting salary. He thought about it for a while—his wife is an Ameri-

can girl who came from one of the towns around Boston—but then decided he'd be happier back in Mexico working with his father. I still hear from him occasionally.

"All in all," Dr. Smith added, "I think you could say that Giminez was a damn good doctor who wasn't looking for any trouble but just stumbled into a position that made life rough for him for a while."

"I suppose you could say the same of Ken Edelin," I said.

"I guess you could at that," Dr. Smith answered. "That whole case was a sorry affair."

Homans made many telling points in his attempt to make Giminez' testimony appear to be of questionable validity. For one thing, Giminez' memory of other events related to the Alice Roe abortion was not as definite as his testimony about the clock. He seemed uncertain as to which operating room was the one in which the operation took place. He could not name all the people who were in attendance.

Homans also wondered, if Giminez were watching the clock as the three minutes went by, how he could also be watching Edelin to make certain his hand was not moving. And, since Edelin's hand was presumably deep in Alice Roe's pelvis, how could Giminez actually see Edelin's fingers in the uterus? (He could not, of course; he could only surmise, from lack of motion in the wrist or any visible portion of the hand, that the fingers were at rest.)

Homans also pointed out that for Edelin to stare for three minutes at the clock on the wall, he would have had to twist his neck almost to a right angle or else turn his back to the patient—assuming the clocks were in their usual positions on the usual wall.

And this was another telling point raised to discredit Giminez' testimony. According to some of the nurses and engineers who were responsible for maintenance at Boston City

148

Hospital, the clock in the operating room where Alice Roe's hysterotomy was performed may have been either broken or actually removed for repair on the day Edelin was operating on Alice Roe. Ordinarily there should have been two clocks on the wall—as there are in most operating rooms. One is an ordinary clock, usually with a second hand. The other is a clock that functions like a stop watch; the nurse pulls a switch at the beginning of an operation—or of any procedure during an operation that the surgeon wishes to time—and when that operation or procedure is over, a second switch is pulled to stop the clock. After noting how long the procedure took the nurse pulls a switch and resets all the hands of the clock at twelve. (I sometimes use such a clock when I am trying to stop bleeding in the abdomen by applying pressure to an oozing surface. Otherwise, I know that I will underestimate the two or three minutes during which I intend to apply pressure.)

Were both clocks, one clock or no clocks present in the operating room when Edelin was operating? Even after all the testimony and noting all the repair records that were made available, a definite answer to that question was simply not possible. It seemed to me, after reading the testimony, that even Flanagan and Homans were willing to agree that absolute proof was lacking. Flanagan certainly felt Giminez was telling the truth and that at least one clock was on the wall, but unfortunately, Boston City Hospital's records being the mess that most city hospital records are, he could not use these records as reliable documentation.

Edelin's claim that he did not stop and watch a clock for three minutes was supported by Ellyn Curtis, the "circulating" nurse who worked with the operating team during the hysterotomy. A circulating nurse is one whose job it is to bring sterile instruments that may be necessary but aren't already available to the scrub nurse, to count sponges before the procedure begins and again just before the uterus and abdomen are closed and to take from the doctor or scrub nurse

149

the specimen removed during the operation—in this case the fetus, a placenta and amniotic sac. Here is her pertinent testimony.

> **Q.** (by **Homans**) Now, Miss Curtis, whether or not in reference to Operating Room 2 you remember the presence or the absence of either or both of two clocks at any time in 1973?
> **A.** There was no clock on the wall in Operating Room 2 at that time.
> **Q.** When you refer to a clock, do you mean a timer or a clock?
> **A.** As I recall, the timer wasn't working, but the clock was missing from the wall.

And then, a little later, this exchange took place:

> **Q.** What did you see Dr. Edelin do, if anything, concerning looking at the clock in the operating room while he was doing the operation?
> **A.** He was moving his fingers around the uterus, or I shouldn't say, inside the abdomen.
> **Q.** And what did you see him doing insofar as looking at a clock?
> **A.** He never looked at any clock.

Ms. Curtis also added another factor to the case. Here is her pertinent testimony.

> **Q.** (**Flanagan**) After you say you saw the defendant with his two fingers in there, what next took place?
> **A.** (**Curtis**) He was moving his fingers around.
> **Q.** All right, and how long did he move his fingers around?
> **A.** Oh, maybe for about a minute.

150

Q. And then what did he do?
A. Then he asked me to get Dr. Charles. [Dr. David
Charles, the chief of obstetrics]
Q. All right. Did you go get Dr. Charles?
A. Yes, I did.

She then testified that it only took about five seconds to get
Dr. Charles, who was in the coffee room about thirty feet
from the operating room. When she came back, she said, Dr.
Edelin's fingers were still in the abdomen. (She could not
swear they were in the uterus since, naturally, she could not
see them, but she assumed, because of the instruments Edelin
had already used, that he had opened the uterus and his
fingers were inside it.) After Charles had arrived, Flanagan
asked her, "What next took place?"

A. He talked with Dr. Charles for a second.
Q. And then what happened?
A. I didn't hear the conversation. Dr. Charles left the
operating room.
Q. All right. How long did they talk?
A. Just for a couple of seconds.

When I read Ellyn Curtis' testimony, it seemed odd to me
that, since Edelin had neglected to mention Charles' visit to
the operating room, Newman Flanagan hadn't subpoenaed
Charles to ask him about the conversation that had taken
place between Edelin and him. It seemed to me that Edelin, in
omitting from his testimony any reference to his sending for
Charles, had left the implication that testimony regarding the
conversation might be damaging to Edelin.

On May 31, 1977, I phoned Newman Flanagan at his home
to ask him why he hadn't subpoenaed Charles. "We would
have loved to have questioned him," Flanagan said, "but unfortunately for us Charles was under indictment for the

151

'grave-robber' case, and we knew he could and would take the fifth if we questioned him about this one. The defense was willing to call him if we'd agree to limit our questions as they wanted us to limit them, but of course I wouldn't stipulate to that. So we had to let him off. Though, just like you, we thought it was curious that Edelin failed to mention sending for him."*

I also learned, from conversations with representatives of the district attorney's office, that they felt Ellyn Curtis was considerably underestimating the time she spent getting Dr. Charles and the time he spent in conversation with Edelin. I agree. It is virtually impossible to leave an operating room, walk even thirty feet to another room and return with a doctor in five seconds. Not even if both parties ran as fast as they could, which seems unlikely since Dr. Edelin hardly seemed to consider speed an urgent matter in this hysterotomy case. It's also unlikely that Dr. Charles would be wearing an operating mask while sitting in the coffee room. He would have to put one on, or at least pull up and tie one, if it were dangling from his neck, before entering the operating room.

Nor is it likely that any conversation between two people would be completed in two seconds. It seems apparent that Ellyn Curtis was estimating time the way most of us do when we say something like "Be with you in a second." I would suspect the entire Dr. Charles episode must have taken at least a few minutes, which lends support to the idea that Edelin's hand was in Alice Roe's uterus longer than he estimated was the case.

What did Dr. Charles and Edelin talk about? Since neither has chosen to relate the conversation (at least as of June 23,

---

*Homans gives a different explanation for Dr. Charles' failure to testify. When I questioned Homans on August 19, 1977, he told me, "I wanted Dr. Charles to testify, but his [Charles'] lawyer wouldn't let him. I never could understand why he wouldn't let him."

1977, as I write this), we can only guess. Perhaps Edelin just wanted a suggestion as to how he might safely extend the uterine incision in order to get the fetus out. However, the district attorney's office speculates, and admittedly they have as yet nothing to base this on other than Edelin's and Charles' silence, that Edelin probably said something like "This baby is big and he's alive. What shall I do?" And that Charles answered, "Just wait and make sure he's dead when you take him out." Perhaps it is unfair to Edelin and Charles to even speculate that that may have been the gist of their conversation. But in the absence of any statement to the contrary by either person, the district attorney's office is free to interpret their silence in any way that seems reasonable. And to them such an exchange seems not only reasonable but likely. Here is a quote from the district attorney's reply to the defendant's appeal of the final verdict:

> The defendant must have known that there were legal risks involved in his conduct toward the child. Not to have delayed would have increased the likelihood of the live birth of an unwanted child, and to have killed the child thereafter would clearly have been homicide. The defendant must have known that his only protection was to attempt to make sure that the child was stillborn. Since it was alive when the procedure began, he had to act affirmatively to kill it lest it survive. He could not have been factually unaware of the legal risks involved if a child was born and he neglected it.

14

Which brings us to some critical legal niceties of the Edelin case.

It is essential that we remember that on October 3, 1973, there were no laws regulating abortion in Massachusetts. The Supreme Court of the United States had, as you will recall, summarized its findings in the *Roe* v. *Wade* case as follows:

(a) For the stage prior to approximately the end of the first trimester, the abortion decision and its effectuation must be left to the medical judgment of the pregnant woman's attending physician.

(b) For the stage subsequent to approximately the end of the first trimester, the State, in promoting its interests in the health of the mother, may, if it chooses, regulate the abortion procedure in ways that are reasonably related to maternal health.

(c) For the stage subsequent to viability, the State, in promoting its interest in the potentiality of human life,

may, if it chooses, regulate and even proscribe abortion except where it is necessary, in appropriate medical judgment, for the preservation of the life or health of the mother.

Although the Supreme Court did not define "viability," it did, in an extensive review of the historical definitions of the term, say that "Viability is usually placed at about seven months (twenty-eight weeks) but may occur earlier, even at twenty-four weeks." This statement was taken from a standard obstetrical textbook by Hellman and Pritchard.

However, it was not until August 2, 1974, that Massachusetts passed laws regulating or restricting abortion. Theoretically, from January 22, 1973, until August 2, 1974, it was legal to abort a woman at any time during her pregnancy, even including the final few weeks when her child-fetus would, admittedly, be indisputably capable of survival outside the uterus.

Which means that Kenneth Edelin was clearly within his legal rights in performing an abortion on Alice Roe, even if, as the prosecution tried to establish, the fetus were twenty-four weeks old and potentially viable.

However, as we have said before, manslaughter does not have to be a crime of commission. As the prosecution said in its reply to Edelin's appeal of his conviction (p. 53), "The common law of manslaughter also makes criminal the neglect of a child that results in death:

. . . if [the] death is the direct consequence of the malicious omission of the performance of a duty (as of a mother to nourish her infant child) this is a case of murder. If the omission was not malicious and arose from negligence only, it is a case of manslaughter. . . . This statement is supported by numerous authorities. . . . [court's collection of authorities omitted.] . . ."

156

THE BABY IN THE BOTTLE

The defense did not argue with this definition of manslaughter.

However, for Edelin to have been guilty of manslaughter, the Roe baby would have had to have been alive when it was removed from its mother's uterus. Even the prosecution conceded this when, in arguing against Edelin's appeal, they quoted from two authorities on whose words the common law—which was then the only pertinent abortion law in Massachusetts—was based. Here are the two pertinent quotes.

Sir Edward Coke, writing in the seventeenth century, stated the rule to be less severe [than one in force in 1327], but insisted that injuring an unborn child was homicide if the child died as a result of the injury after having been born alive:

If a woman be quick with childe, and by a Potion or otherwise killeth it in her wombe; or if a man beat her, whereby the child dieth in her body, and she is delivered of a dead childe, this is a great misprision, and no murder; but if the childe be born alive, and dieth of the Potion, battery or other cause, this is murder: for in the law it is accounted a reasonable creative in verum natura; when it is born alive. E. Coke, "Third Institute," 50 (1644)

Sir William Blackstone, in his eighteenth century commentaries, confirms Coke:

To kill a child in its mother's womb is now no murder, but a great misprision: but if the child be born alive and dieth by reason of the portion (sic) or bruises it receives in the womb, it seems by the better opinion, to be murdered in such as administered or gave them. W. Blackstone, "Commentaries on the Law of England," 198 (1769)

* * *

William A. Nolen, M.D.

What all this meant, to both the prosecution and the defense, was that if on opening Alice Roe's uterus, Kenneth Edelin found a live baby (as the prosecution contended), and if he detached the placenta so that the baby would be deprived of oxygen and, in a matter of three or four minutes, die of suffocation (as, again, the prosecution contended), that Kenneth Edelin was still not guilty of murder, manslaughter or any other crime provided he did not remove the child from the uterus until it was dead. In the eyes of the law this fetus-child-baby was not "born" nor was it a human being (with all the rights to which a human being is entitled, including protection from murder or manslaughter) until it was outside its mother's uterus. This may seem to the average person like illogical hairsplitting—it certainly seems that way to me—but on October 3, 1973, in Massachusetts, that was the law.

In *Roe* v. *Wade* the Supreme Court said,

The Constitution does not define "person" in so many words. Section I of the Fourteenth Amendment contains three references to "person." The first, in defining "citizens" speaks of "persons born or naturalized in the United States." The word also appears both in the Due Process Clause and in the Equal Protection Clause. "Person" is used in other places in the Constitution: [these are then cited]. But in nearly all these instances, the use of the word is such that it only has application postnatally. None indicates, with any assurance, that it has any possible prenatal application.

All this, together with our observation that throughout the major portion of the 19th century prevailing legal abortion practices were far freer than they are today, persuades us that the word "person" as used in the Fourteenth Amendment does not include the unborn.

158

* * *

In other words, the decision that a fetus is not a person is not one that has been inscribed on stone and passed down to us by Moses. It is, rather, a decision made, on the basis of tradition, by nine Supreme Court justices struggling to find a remedy for a very difficult problem. They might, if they had so chosen, have decided that a fetus, either from the moment of its conception or after twenty weeks or after detachment from its mother (though still in the uterus) was a person. Their decision that a fetus would be considered a "person" only after it had been removed from the womb was an arbitrary one and certainly one with which reasonable people may logically disagree.

There was no major disagreement as to what happened after Edelin finally removed the fetus—or baby, depending on which label you prefer—from Alice Roe's uterus. He looked at the baby (it immediately became a baby as soon as it was removed from the uterus) and saw neither breathing nor motion of an extremity. He put his hand on the child's chest for three to five seconds (he estimated) and then put the baby in a metal pan which the scrub nurse was holding. Edelin then turned his attention back to Alice Roe. He wiped the inner wall of her uterus to remove any amniotic sac that might have been left behind; he took a clamp and spread the mouth of the uterus, so that clots or residual membranes left behind could easily drain out; and he began to close the uterus.

In the meantime Ellyn Curtis took the fetus, and a few minutes later the placenta (which was removed after the fetus), and put them in cardboard boxes that were sent, after the operation was completed, to the pathology department, where they were delivered to Dr. Frank Fallico. He looked at and weighed the fetus and found that it weighed 600 grams. The placenta weighed 170 grams. He could see no fetal abnormali-

ties. Since the fetus came with a tag, signed by Edelin, that said it was twenty-two weeks of age, he did not dissect the fetus. Hospital regulations said that any fetus over twenty weeks of age was not to be dissected. The resident's job was simply to weigh the fetus, look at it and note any abnormalities, notify his superior that the fetus had been brought to the pathology department, and then put the fetus in a two-quart plastic container containing a preservative solution of 10 percent formalin. The fetus was then to be transferred to the mortuary.

Dr. Fallico was examined and cross-examined at some length—particularly, it seems, because he had not put the fetal weight on his report till two days after the fetus had been delivered to the surgical pathology department. He explained that he had not recorded the weight because he was not certain he should have done so. In any event, the fetus in its two-quart plastic container with a screw-on cap was eventually transferred to the mortuary. In December 1973, as we already know, at Newman Flanagan's request Dr. George Curtis went to the mortuary and found the jar that contained the preserved fetus.

15

We now must try to answer the crucial question in the Edelin case—was the fetus alive when Kenneth Edelin removed it from Alice Roe's uterus?

Edelin had said no. He looked at the fetus when he removed it and did not see it breathe or move. He placed his hand on the chest of the fetus for three to five seconds and felt no heartbeat. Having neither seen nor felt any sign of life, he turned the fetus over to a nurse and went back to work on his patient.

Was that, both from the moral and, particularly, the legal perspective, an adequate search for signs of fetal life? The prosecution didn't think so. After all, by the time it was removed from the uterus, the fetus had been under anesthesia for more than a half hour and, as Edelin conceded, this might have affected the fetus' activity. The fetus had been under anesthesia just as its mother had, and when recovering from an anesthetic, a patient is apt to take shallow, irregular

breaths and move sluggishly. Here is an exchange between Flanagan and Edelin.

> Q. **(Flanagan)** Isn't it common knowledge in the medical field that when a woman receives some type of drug to put her to sleep in an operation where she is pregnant that that drug goes to the fetus?
> A. **(Edelin)** Yes, sir.
> Q. And causes the fetus to be sleepy or drowsy, or has a similar effect on the fetus as it does on the mother?
> A. It could, yes, sir.

Edelin then said that the anesthesia would not have had any effect on the fetal heartbeat, after which Flanagan asked:

> Q. Did you make any determination other than this heartbeat examination of three to five seconds where you've put your hand on the chest?
> Other than that, did you make any other determination as to whether or not the subject was alive or dead?
> A. Other than observing it for spontaneous movement and for respiratory movements, feeling the left anterior chest wall for heartbeat, no.
> Q. Are there other means available to determine it?
> A. Whether the fetus was alive or not?
> Q. Yes.
> A. Yes.
> Q. Did you do any of them?
> A. No.

When Dr. Jeffrey Gould, director of newborn services at Boston City Hospital testified, he stated that a child is live-born, by the World Health Organization definition, if it has either a single heartbeat or a single respiration within the first

minute of life. Clearly, by his own testimony, Dr. Edelin did not spend enough time examining the Roe fetus to determine, by these standards, whether or not it was liveborn. If he had been extremely interested in the fetus' life or health, he might have gotten an electroencephalogram (to see if there was any brain activity) or an electrocardiogram (to learn if there were any electrical impulses passing through the heart). But these were extraordinary things that no obstetrician or pediatrician would have felt compelled to do. The point that the prosecution wanted to make and did was that Edelin did not even take the ordinary, minimal steps one might take if he wanted to know if the fetus showed any signs of life. Neither Edelin nor anyone else whom he might have asked to do so took a stethoscope and listened for one minute to see if they could hear the fetus' heartbeat or hear it take a breath. Three to five seconds of observation and palpation were clearly not enough to say with certainty that Alice Roe's child was stillborn.

(As I mentioned earlier in this book, the defense and prosecution haggled at great length over what to call whatever was in Alice Roe's uterus. I have used "fetus," "subject," "baby," child" and "products of conception" at various times, with no predetermined plan. I have, of course, stuck to the wording of the trial transcript when I have quoted from it.)

As long as we are discussing terminology, I should point out that Edelin testified he never used the word "baby" when discussing the products of conception with a mother seeking an abortion. He apparently felt, and understandably so, that that word is an emotionally charged one that might make abortion a more difficult emotional crisis for the woman than it would be if they referred to the contents of her uterus as a "fetus" or "subject."

And Dr. Jeffrey Gould, in testifying about newborns, had this to say in answer to one of Homans' questions.

A. In general, people working in nurseries don't refer to

163

babies under 900 or 1000 grams as "babies" or "infants" until these babies show signs of long-term survival.

Q. What are they called?

A. A variety of things, usually a fetus, or a—it's very hard to say. They kind of avoid the question because it's very difficult for them to deal with infants such as this until they are sure that there is a possibility of survival.

Obviously, whether we are doctor, nurse or lay person, some words are charged with emotion by our past experiences. Most of us, when we use the word "baby," see in our mind's eye a chubby, smiling infant laughing in a crib—and all the hairsplitting definitions in the world won't enable us to erase that image.

We will return to the definition and problem of determining "viability" later, but for the moment we must deal, as did the prosecution, with the question of whether or not the fetus removed from Alice Roe was "alive," by any reasonable definition of that word, at the time Edelin removed it from her uterus.

By the time of the trial it was obviously too late to listen for a heartbeat or order an electroencephalogram. The only course the prosecution could follow was to try and establish the probability that at the time the Roe baby was removed from the uterus it was alive. (Once this being was out of the uterus, both prosecution and defense agreed it was, by definition, a baby; the dispute in terminology dealt only with the name that should be applied while it was in the uterus.)

To "prove" as best he could that the Roe baby was not stillborn, Flanagan had to rely primarily on the autopsy results. Dr. George Curtis, who performed the autopsy, reported on the weight of the heart, the adrenal glands, the thyroid and, of course, on the weight of the fetus itself. He claimed that, after

approximately three-and-a-half months in the formalin solution, the fetus weighed 700 grams.

Now, naturally the question arose as to which weight was the correct one: the 600 grams Dr. Fallico had testified the baby weighed when he first received it in the morgue or the 700 grams Curtis claimed the fetus weighed at the time he did the autopsy.

Flanagan tried to suggest that the 600 gram weight recorded by Fallico was in error. First, since Fallico had, by his own admission, not written down the fetal weight till two days after he had weighed the fetus, it was possible, Flanagan implied, that he might have forgotten the actual weight or confused the weight of the Roe fetus with that of some other fetus. After all, fetuses were arriving at the pathology department with relative frequency. When asked about how many other fetuses Fallico had examined on October 2, October 3 and October 4, he repeatedly testified, "I don't recall."

Flanagan also hinted that Fallico might be lying to protect his friend Edelin. Fallico had flown to Boston from Minnesota, where he was a resident in pathology at the time of the trial. Here is the exchange between Fallico and Flanagan.

Q. (Flanagan) You have talked to Dr. Edelin, haven't you, about what you were going to testify to?
A. (Fallico) No.
Q. You didn't? What did you do Saturday with Dr. Edelin?
A. Rode in from the airport with him.
Q. And just talked about the weather?
A. Yes. We did discuss the weather.
Q. The heat was on here. It's a lot hotter than out in Minnesota, isn't it?
Mr. Homans: Objection, your Honor.
The Court: Wait a moment. Just a moment. Strike the entire colloquy.

165

William A. Nolen, M.D.

* * *

Flanagan had scored a point. It was possible, of course, that all Dr. Fallico and Dr. Edelin talked about was the weather as they drove in from the airport to the city where Fallico was to testify in Edelin's trial, but I doubt that that was the case, and I suspect the jury doubted it, too. (Which does not mean that I think Fallico and Edelin planned any deception; I don't. I simply think it would be completely unnatural not to at least mention the trial, a subject that must have been at the forefront of both their minds.)

The importance of determining the true weight of the Roe baby was related to its chances of survival. Although there is in the medical literature a report of one child (called the Munro baby) who weighed 397 grams at birth, and survived and thrived, it is generally accepted that for a baby to have a reasonable chance to survive more than twenty-eight days, and leave the hospital to go home, it must weigh at least 1000 grams. (The Munro baby was born, unattended by a physician, and was weighed in a grocery story on a grocery scale. For these reasons, some obstetricians question the accuracy of this report.)

However there is no question that, although the odds are against it, an infant weighing 700 grams has a chance of surviving, even if we assume that survival means living for at least twenty-eight days in the hospital and then going home in a healthy condition with a normal life expectancy. There were several expert witnesses who testified as to chances of survival, but I shall quote only one, Dr. Schuyler G. Kohl, who was called as a witness by the defense.

Dr. Kohl is a professor of obstetrics and gynecology at the College of Medicine, State University of New York Downstate Medical Center. He has a master's degree in biostatistics and epidemiology and a doctor of public health degree, both from Columbia University. His particular area of specialty is in biostatistics and epidemiology of obstetrics and gynecolo-

166

gy. He's the director of an organization called the Obstetrical Statistical Cooperative, which collects data from thirty-five hospitals across the United States. Although Dr. Kohl's testimony ran for several pages, here is that part of the testimony which applied particularly to the Edelin case.

> **Q. (Homans)** Dr. Kohl, I ask you again, sir, would you tell us how many infants in the 700 to 799 gram area between 1961 and 1972 were discharged home alive from the Kings County Hospital.
>
> **A.** Six.
>
> **Q.** And how many total births in that period of 1961 to 1972 were there in the area of 700 to 799 grams, sir?
>
> **A.** 283.
>
> **Q.** Now, sir, with respect to the area of 600 to 699 grams, I ask you how many infants who were born alive were discharged alive to go home, sir?
>
> **A.** One.
>
> **Q.** And I ask you how many was the total of infants in that range, that is, 699 grams?
>
> **A.** 359.

The importance of knowing the weight of the Roe baby is obvious. If the baby weighed 400 grams, its chance of surviving, based on all medical reports through 1972, was nil. (With the possible, questionable exception of the Munro baby.)

If the Roe baby weighed only 600 grams, then, at least according to figures compiled between 1961 and 1972, its chances of survival were one in 359. If it weighed between 700 and 799 grams, its chances of survival were 6 out of 283.

One point I think Newman Flanagan might have made and didn't was that the chances of survival for an infant weighing between 600 and 700 grams (the presumed weight of the Roe baby) were, in October 1973, undoubtedly much greater than the figures Dr. Kohl had collected. After all, his figures were

167

collected over an eleven-year period going back to 1961. In 1961 the equipment and knowledge available to keep a premature infant alive were primitive in comparison to what was available in 1973. So the figures from the early period included in the study would tend to weigh the odds against survival. In fact, at the time the Roe baby was born, some specialists in care of the newborn placed the chances of survival—based on a presumed weight between 600 and 700 grams—at about 1 percent. Not good, but far from as bad as Dr. Kohl's testimony suggested.

Now, back to the question of weight. Did the Roe baby weigh 600 grams and was the weight of 700 grams, recorded by Dr. Curtis, a distortion caused by 3½ months of immersion in a 10 percent formalin solution?

According to Dr. John Ward, a pathologist at the University of Pittsburgh School of Medicine and an associate clinical professor of the School of Pharmacology at Duquesne University in Pittsburgh, the formalin solution, rather than adding to the weight of the fetus, would tend to decrease it. Here is his pertinent testimony.

Q. (Flanagan) Now, Doctor, assume that the subject of this particular matter was fixed in formalin, in ten percent formalin, do you have an opinion as to whether or not the subject in a period of approximately three and a half to four months whether the subject would gain or lose weight.

A. (Ward) The subject would lose weight. . . .

This is due to the fact that immediately upon death the fetus loses weight. Therefore, if a tissue is fixed after death, one assumes that this weight immediately is less because of the death of the tissue; and further because of the dehydrating effects of formalin the tissue would even be further reduced from its normal weight.

168

* * *

Dr. Ward also said that, on the basis of the organ weights and fetal measurements recorded by Dr. Curtis, he would estimate the age of the Roe baby at twenty-six weeks, though Dr. Curtis had estimated its age at about twenty-three weeks.

As far as the fetal weight is concerned, I suspect that Dr. Fallico's recording of 600 grams is less reliable than is Dr. Curtis' of 700 grams.

Dr. Fallico, as you may recall, waited two days before he wrote down the weight of the fetus as he remembered it. In the meantime he had examined other fetuses which he had also, presumably, weighed. By the time the two days had elapsed I suspect that Dr. Fallico probably could not remember what weight went with which fetus. And since by that time he may have suspected that the Roe baby might prove to be a legal problem—he must have known by then that no one at Boston City Hospital was willing to sign the baby's death certificate for fear of being involved in a legal controversy—Fallico may well have felt that, since he couldn't absolutely remember what the fetus weighed, it might be advisable to attribute to it one of the lighter weights he remembered from his recent work. A fetus that was relatively light was apt to prove less controversial than a heavy one.

Dr. Curtis, on the other hand, was in a position where he knew with certainty he was dealing with a baby that was going to be the source of controversy. After all, the examination was being done at the request of the district attorney's office and that, in all probability, meant trouble. Moreover, it was possible, perhaps likely, that another doctor would check the fetal weight after Curtis recorded it. He had to be accurate.

And, based on the testimony of others, the weight Curtis recorded—700 grams—was probably lighter than the fetus' weight immediately after birth. Even Homans pointed out in his argument against admitting a photo of the fetus as evidence that after three months in formalin the "wrinkled skin"

169

of the fetus distorted the appearance of the fetus as it had been at the time of the hysterotomy. "Wrinkled skin" is considered a sign of dehydration, so that, in effect, Homans' argument lent support to the idea that the fetus probably weighed more than 700 grams at birth and so had a potentially greater chance of survival than that for which Flanagan was arguing.

As to whether or not this fetus was alive when it was delivered from its mother's uterus, we must again use indirect evidence—the postmortem examination of the lungs.

Here there was conflicting expert testimony. Dr. George Curtis, who performed the autopsy, and Dr. Ward, who reviewed the microscopic slides Curtis had made of pieces taken from the lung, both felt that the baby had breathed air. Curtis said he could not be certain the baby had breathed air while still in the mother's uterus or after it had been removed from the mother. Ward felt the baby had breathed air after it had been removed from the mother, but he based his conclusion on his assumption that a baby could not take a breath while inside a uterus, an assumption Homans pointed out was wrong.

Dr. Shirley Driscoll, a pathologist at the Lying-In Division of the Boston Hospital for Women, examined the lungs and concluded that the fetus had breathed in amniotic fluid but not air. Her testimony involved some very technical matters about protein and its distribution in the air spaces of the lung, but the essence of her testimony, as the defense summarized it in appealing the case, was that Dr. Driscoll found "no circular bubble-like spaces" which would have been present "if there had been some gas, air or oxygen in these lungs."

After reading the testimony on both sides of this question, I conclude it was a standoff. The baby may or may not have

breathed and, if he did take a breath, it may have been either while still in the uterus or after removal.

If the baby did take a breath outside its mother's body, then—as we've noted—it was "liveborn" according to the World Health Organization definition of liveborn. However, the American College of Obstetricians and Gynecologists defines a liveborn infant as follows:

Liveborn Infant. Liveborn infant is a fetus, irrespective of its gestational age, that after complete expulsion or extraction from the mother shows evidence of life— that is, heartbeats or respirations. Heartbeats are to be distinguished from several transient cardiac contractions; respirations are to be distinguished from fleeting respiratory efforts or gasps. . . .

Homans and Edelin, without conceding that the Roe baby took even one fleeting gasp outside its mother, felt that even if that were true—even if it did take one or two gasps—it certainly never breathed in a way that would enable anyone to define it as "liveborn" according to the American College of Obstetricians and Gynecologists definition of that term. The defense wanted Judge McGuire to instruct the jury that they should define breathing according to this definition rather than that of the World Health Organization's definition. He refused to do so.

I would agree with the defense that, from the evidence, it would seem certain the baby did not breathe, except perhaps fleetingly, and so was not liveborn on the basis of breathing, according to the more rigorous definition of the American College of Obstetricians and Gynecologists. On the other hand, there was certainly no evidence that, if the baby did make at least one successful if feeble attempt to breathe, Edelin or anyone else in the operating room—who would and

171

could have acted on his instructions—worked on the infant to help it skip from one or two irregular, spasmodic gasps to a rhythmic, effective breathing pattern.

Anyone who has ever delivered a baby suffering from anoxia—whether that anoxia has been caused by separation of the placenta, anesthesia, or any of several other causes—knows that with a few minutes of help from a nurse or a doctor and perhaps with the use of stimulant drugs or mechanical aids to respiration, a baby who would otherwise die can be kept alive. All that is necessary is to give the struggling infant the help it needs to fight off the effects of the anoxia—or, in fact, the help it needs to survive till the effects of the anesthetic wear off spontaneously. But the doctor or nurse who fights for that baby's life must begin the fight as soon as the child is born; otherwise the anoxia will damage other organs—the brain in particular—and the child's condition will deteriorate and quickly become irreversible.

Of all the testimony regarding an infant's chances of survival, I, as a physician, thought the most effective was, or should have been, that of Dr. Jeffrey Gould. Dr. Gould was called as an expert witness for the defense, but it was his testimony under cross-examination by Newman Flanagan that I found most interesting. Here is the appropriate exchange; in it, Flanagan and Gould are discussing the treatment of newborn premature infants that are brought to the nursery which Dr. Gould directs.

> Q. And Doctor, when an infant is brought to you, you do all that you can for that infant, is that correct, Doctor?
>
> A. All that is appropriate to do for the infant.
>
> Q. And who then makes the determination of whether the infant lives?

A. The determination, I think, is made by the infant, and the doctor helps.

Q. The doctor determines whether or not the baby lives?

A. No, I think that the infant determines whether or not the infant lives, and the doctor helps.

Q. So that the infant decides or determines whether he lives or not, is that correct?

A. That would be correct in current pediatric usage.

Your Honor, may I clarify that, because that's a very important—

The Court: You may answer each question as fully as you feel that that question needs to be answered.

The Witness: All right.

Q. Have you finished?

A. No, I haven't answered that.

I think that it's important to express exactly what I am talking about.

If you have an infant at 700 grams, and if you look at the studies or look at doctors' experiences, those infants that lived are infants who present breathing, are infants who present with heart rates, are infants who present with a little bit of tone. In other words, these infants look as though they are fighting for life, and the pediatrician or the obstetrician or whoever is there intervenes.

Now, it's true that many of these infants get attached to $20,000 worth of equipment, but this is after the determination has been seen that this is an infant who is fighting for its life. You have no trouble telling the rare 700-gram infant that has a chance, because he is there, and it is extremely rare, because he is there and you can see him gasping, and you can see tone in his arms. And you can see indications that this infant is struggling for life.

173

William A. Nolen, M.D.

It is at that point that the doctor intervenes.

Now, on the other hand, I would like to contrast that with the 700-gram infant that has a very, very rare chance of survival, and this would be an infant who is born, who is a liveborn infant, because he has a heartbeat. Okay. That heartbeat may be two beats per minute. It's a liveborn infant because he has a breathing, and that breathing may be one gasp in the first thirty seconds. The infant is blue. The infant has no tone. The infant is already starting to hemorrhage. These infants don't survive, and they tell you this right from the beginning.

The physician, faced with an infant like this, perhaps, will try to stimulate, will try to give a little bit of oxygen, and look for a favorable response. If there is a favorable response, then that infant, even though the outlook is so incredibly bad, will, perhaps, put that infant—and attach that infant to approximately $15,000 to $18,000 worth of equipment, and try and try and try.

In general, results with an infant that looks that bad have been very, very disappointing. So again I would like to come back to the point that in part the infant decides whether he is viable, in that as you look at the infant the viable infant is really moving, it is obvious.

On the other hand, I must state that the likelihood of a child from 600 to 700 grams of looking like this is 99.6 percent, or only 1 infant out of 250 would at the age range that Mr. Flanagan asked me about, only 1 infant in 250 will survive between 600 and 700 grams, will look viable as the pediatrician is called. To me, 1 out of 250 is miraculous, really.

Mr. Flanagan: I would ask that the latter part be stricken, your Honor.

174

Mr. Homans: I am not sure what the latter part is, your Honor.

The Court: The word "miraculous" may be stricken.

I suppose I found this testimony particularly interesting and effective because in essence Dr. Gould was dealing with that very nebulous entity, the will to live. The will to live is indefinable, but every physician can spot it when it's present and is quickly and uncomfortably aware of its absence. When adults, particularly the elderly, have it, the doctor, nurses and aides sense this and know that that patient has a chance—may survive—if everyone works hard to help him or her. When the spark isn't there, we sense that, too, and know that no matter how hard we work, the patient will probably die. Every experienced doctor has had patients who have survived who should not have, when we consider how critically ill they are. Their survival is, as Dr. Gould said of these premature infants, something they—not the doctor—achieve.

What is disturbing in the Roe case is that, by his own admission, Edelin made no attempt to see if the child had that spark. As Gould said, the will to live isn't always immediately apparent; it becomes obvious only if "the physician will try to stimulate, will try to give a little bit of oxygen, and look for a favorable response."

The Roe baby wasn't given this bit of provocation that might—just might—have shown it had the will to live. Why? The answer is distressingly simple. No one wanted the Roe baby to live.

16

Of all the disputes between the prosecution and the defense, probably the most bitter was over the admission as evidence of photographs of the Roe baby. Here is the defense's summary of their argument as presented in their appeal:

Over strenuous objection of defense counsel the prosecution was permitted to introduce into evidence a photograph of the dead fetus which was (and is) utterly shocking and inflammatory to the mind of a lay person. It pictured the dead fetus, its skin wrinkled and loose after four months in formaldehyde, lying as if discarded on a metal work bench or photographic stand. The true nature of this photograph and its potential for inflammatory and prejudicial impact upon the jury can only be assessed by examining it.

Dr. Edelin, through his counsel, took the position that the photographs of the fetus: (1) had "no relevance" in this case, (2) were "inflammatory," (3) were, if at all

177

relevant, cumulative in proving the issues already dealt with in the autopsy of Dr. Curtis and (4) that their "probative value," if any, was not "sufficient to overcome the inflammatory nature of these photos. . . ."

The Commonwealth, on the other hand, took the position (1) that this evidence is very, very material to the issue of whether in fact there ever was a baby boy, alive or dead; (2) that it would corroborate Dr. Giminez's testimony "that in fact this particular baby [sic] was removed from the patient in this case" and, in rebuttal to argument of counsel for Dr. Edelin, (3) that the photographs had probative value as to "viability and gestational age of the deceased," and (4) that they would corroborate and aid the jury in understanding the details and testimony of the medical examiner.

Over the objection and exception of the defendant Exhibit 9 (a photograph of the Roe baby) was admitted in evidence, according to the trial judge, "for such assistance, if any, it offers to you." The trial judge did not specify any issue upon which it was admitted other than to say that the defendant was on trial for "manslaughter, which is the killing of a person." With a caution concerning refraining from "emotional" response and from viewing the photograph in an "inflammatory" context, the trial judge concluded his "limiting" instructions by saying:

"You are to view it [the photograph] to determine whether it offers any assistance to you, that is, whether it has any evidential value on a material issue in this case. That's the only purpose for which this picture is introduced."

Should Judge McGuire have admitted the picture as evidence? I think so. After all, the jury—as Homans pointed out—was made up of lay people, not doctors or nurses. Most

probably did not have any idea what a twenty- to twenty-six-week-old fetus looked like, and, it seems to me, they had not only a right to but a need for that information. They were being asked to decide whether this "subject" which had been removed from Alice Roe's uterus might have at least a remote chance to survive and have a "meaningful life." Here is the way Flanagan referred to the photo in his closing argument to the jury:

> But let us get back again to the facts in this case. He [Edelin] tells you that he took out the fetus—the subject. Take a look at the picture of the subject. Is this just a specimen? You tell us what it is. Look at the picture. Show it to anybody. What would they tell you it was? Use your common sense when you go to your jury deliberation room and humanize that. Are you speaking about a blob, a big bunch of mucus, or what are we talking about here?
>
> Subjects?
>
> I respectfully submit we're talking about an independent human being that the Commonwealth of Massachusetts must protect as well as anybody else in this courtroom including the defendant.

There is no doubt that Homans should have fought vigorously against the admission of the photograph; and if by "inflammatory" he meant, as I suppose he did, that the photo tended to inflame the jurors because after seeing it they would tend to think "This fetus is a real, living child," then it was undoubtedly inflammatory.

But putting legalities aside, as I can do in writing this book, is there anything intrinsically wrong in showing the jurors a picture of a "subject" who has been, supposedly, the victim of manslaughter? I think not. This "subject" looked like a baby because it was, in fact, a baby. Not legally—as long as it

179

was in its mother's uterus—but in every other way. It had a head, legs, arms, genitalia. It looked, in the mother's uterus, exactly as it did one second after it had been removed from that uterus. Yet legally one second it was a fetus and the next a baby. If the picture was inflammatory, and it probably was, then it was inflammatory for a good reason: this was and should have been an inflammatory case.

When I spoke with Dr. Hugh Holtrop in January 1977 and Dr. Ed Lowe in December 1976, I asked them about one matter to which I didn't think Newman Flanagan had given sufficient emphasis during the trial: the fact that not once, except on her admission to the hospital on September 30, 1973, had any doctor or nurse bothered to listen to the heart tones of the fetus in Alice Roe's uterus. It isn't difficult to hear the heart tones of a fetus—ten or fifteen seconds, using either a fetoscope or, often, an ordinary stethoscope, will enable the listener to tell if the fetal heart is beating and if the beat is healthy, i.e., regular and at a normal rate. It seemed particularly odd to me, in view of Homan's argument that the fetus might have died as a result of injury to the fetus from the bloody taps, that Edelin didn't take just a few seconds to listen for the fetal heart tones before he began his hysterotomy.

After all, if the fetus were dead—as Homans and Edelin would have liked the jury to believe was likely—then a hysterotomy would probably, in fact, have been unnecessary. When a fetus dies *in utero*, as sometimes happens even in a pregnancy where no attempt at abortion has been carried out, the obstetrician will not ordinarily intervene. If he waits a few days, the woman will, because of the hormonal changes that follow the death of the fetus, go into labor and deliver the dead baby from below. A hysterotomy, an operation which, like any other, carries some risk to the patient, will have been unnecessary. (In 1974 the national mortality rate from hysterotomy was 270.2 per 100,000 and the incidence of nonfatal

complications, such as hemorrhage and infection, was much higher.)

Both Lowe and Holtrop felt that, in this case, even if the baby were dead, a prompt hysterotomy was the procedure of choice. Both mentioned that infection might have developed in the uterus, as a result of the bloody taps, if a dead fetus were left to deliver spontaneously a few days later. Holtrop also mentioned the psychological strain that prolonged waiting would have on the mother. "After all," he told me, "she wanted to be through with this pregnancy. If the baby were dead, she might have delivered it in a few days, but the emotional strain of those few days of waiting would have been very difficult."

All of which is true. However, it seems to me that simple logic—to say nothing of informed consent—would have made it morally, and possibly legally, obligatory for Dr. Edelin to have listened to Alice Roe's abdomen and—if he heard no heart tones and was able to conclude that in all probability the fetus in her uterus was dead—to discuss the alternatives now open to Ms. Roe, to give her a chance, if she wished, to wait a day or even a few days to see if she would spontaneously deliver the dead baby, thus sparing herself an operation. This alternative was never offered to Ms. Roe.

Why? Admittedly I can only guess at the answer, but I suspect it was not because anyone was particularly concerned about sparing Ms. Roe the minimal risk of a uterine infection (which might have been managed by antibiotics and/or abortion, when and if it developed); nor was it to spare her the psychological strain of waiting a few days to abort the dead fetus spontaneously. After all, that brief psychological trauma, assuming it resulted in the spontaneous delivery of a dead fetus, might—and, in my opinion, probably would—have been less by far than the permanent damage to the psyche of a seventeen-year-old who goes through an operation so that a

181

doctor can remove, for the purpose of terminating its life, the fetus in her womb. The guilt feelings of women who spontaneously give birth to fetuses that have died *in utero* are less intense and of shorter duration than those of women who have had hysterotomies for the purpose of abortion.

If, as Doctors Holtrop and Lowe contended, immediate hysterotomy in Alice Roe's case seemed to them logical for the reasons they advanced, then I think their logic was both faulty and short-sighted. However—and, again, this must only be conjecture, but conjecture based on the evidence—I think that Dr. Edelin, with the blessings of all of his superiors, didn't bother to listen for the fetal heart tones before beginning the operation because he was virtually certain he would hear the regular beat of the fetal heart. He didn't want to hear those fetal heart tones and neither did anyone else. They wanted to proceed, both for Alice Roe's sake and for their own, as if this fetus were already dead, because they knew that what they were about to do was going to produce a dead fetus, even if it meant—as all the evidence at that point suggested—that they were going to have to convert a live fetus to a dead one with their operation.

I want to make it explicit here that when I refer to "their" operation, I do so intentionally. Admittedly, Edelin was the surgeon who performed the hysterotomy and was the individual who had been accused of manslaughter. But Edelin was only the chief resident in Boston City Hospital's department of obstetrics. As chief resident he had, of course, been given the authority to make decisions regarding patient care without, in every case, consulting his superiors—those doctors, independent, board-certified specialists, who worked in either a full- or part-time capacity as consulting doctors at Boston City Hospital. But this was not an ordinary, run-of-the-mill case in which a chief resident would make decisions on his own. This was an unusual and potentially controversial case. Every step of the process that led to the hysterotomy on

182

Alice Roe was condoned, either directly or by failure to raise any objection, by Drs. Holtrop, Penza, Charles and any others who were in any way connected with the case. Edelin was a thirty-five-year-old man who deserved and admitted to responsibility in the Alice Roe case, but, to a large extent, he was acting as the agent of these other doctors, all of whom bore a share of the responsibility for the treatment given Alice Roe. If Edelin were guilty of a crime, they—morally, if not legally—were equally guilty.

(Dr. Ed Lowe, who had not become chief of obstetrics till 1974 and so was not involved in the Edelin case, agreed with that opinion when we talked in December 1976. "I think they left Ken holding the bag," he said. "Holtrop and Charles were just as responsible—in my opinion, even more responsible—than Ken for the way that case was handled. But they were smart enough and experienced enough to duck out. Ken wasn't.")

Newman Flanagan agreed that other doctors might have been just as guilty as Edelin. When I phoned attorney Flanagan on July 12, 1977, he told me, "I got a lot of flak from other doctors for not indicting anyone but Edelin. And I knew the jury might feel the same way—that Edelin was being made to take the rap for these other men. In fact, in my summation to the jury I raised this point. I said, 'Look, if three men rob a store and two of the robbers get away, you don't let off the guy that got caught just because the other two got away. So you shouldn't let Edelin go if you believe he's guilty just because you think other people who are equally guilty are getting off.'

"It's like being stopped for speeding when you see other cars racing by you. It's natural to think, 'Why should I have to pay a fine when these other people don't?' But that's the way the law has to work.

"I thought this Edelin case was something like the Eichmann case. Okay, let's suppose Edelin was following orders.

183

There's a point where you have to say, 'Hey, that order is wrong and I'm not going to obey you.' If you're ordered to commit manslaughter, then you have an obligation to say no.

"But I'll admit that other doctors might well have been indicted along with Edelin."

17

The definitions of "viability" and "meaningful life" were problems with which the prosecution, the defense and the judge wrestled throughout the trial. At the end there was still no consensus as to how they should be defined.

In *Roe* v. *Wade* the Supreme Court elaborated on its decision that the state might, if it wished, actually forbid abortion—except to save the life of the mother—after the fetus had become viable. Here is the appropriate portion of the Supreme Court decision; it was referred to by attorney Homans in the defendant's appeal.

With respect to the State's important and legitimate interest in potential life, the compelling point is at viability. This is so because the fetus then *presumably* has the capability of *meaningful life* outside the mother's womb. State regulations protective of fetal life after viability thus have both logical and biological justifications. If the State is interested in protecting fetal life after viability, it

may go so far as to proscribe abortion during that period except when it is necessary to preserve the life and health of the mother.

After quoting this portion of the decision, Homans went on to say, "Its use of the word 'presumably' and its reference to twenty-eight weeks as the norm indicated an expectation of survival based on more than the tiniest statistical chance."

There were, as might be expected, a variety of definitions of "viability" presented by the expert witnesses for both prosecution and defense. Most of the doctors for the prosecution felt that any baby who was liveborn—i.e., took at least a single breath or had at least one heartbeat during the first minute of life—had to be considered at least potentially viable. For them, this generally meant any baby born after twenty weeks of gestation, and the doctors for the prosecution generally felt that the Roe baby was removed from its mother's uterus after approximately twenty-four weeks of gestation.

The doctors who testified for the defense all felt that the Roe baby was nonviable. Generally, these doctors felt that for a baby to be considered viable it had to meet the World Health Organization's definition of viability, which is survival to the twenty-eighth day after birth.

Which, of course, introduces a Catch-22 element into the matter of viability. Employing the World Health Organization definition, no one can say, at birth, that a child is viable, even if it is born normally after a full thirty-eight weeks of gestation and has all the characteristics of a normal, healthy child, because at birth the child has not demonstrated its ability to survive for twenty-eight days. In fact, if physicians were to adhere strictly to the World Health Organization definition of viability, there would be almost no "viable" children in hospital nurseries, since most normal children go home with their mothers just a few days after birth. Obviously, survival to

twenty-eight days is not meant to be applied as the criterion for viability in general, but only in those cases where an infant is born prematurely and its long-term survival is in doubt.

The Supreme Court justices added another fine source of controversy to their abortion decision when they sought to clarify it by explaining that a state could regulate abortions after the fetus had reached an age where it "presumably has the capability of meaningful life outside the mother's womb."

Just what is a meaningful life? That depends, of course, on one's frame of reference. I have no desire to be facetious, but if we take a cosmic view of man, it is possible to argue that none of us live a meaningful life; certainly, we can argue along with Thoreau that "The mass of men lead lives of quiet desperation." Meaningless lives.

On the other hand, we might go to the other extreme and argue along with many religions, that every life, no matter how brief or apparently inconsequential, is meaningful in the eyes of God. Perhaps the child who is born prematurely and lives only three or four days acts, during its brief sojourn on this earth, as the catalyst that brings its father and mother together in love at a time when that love, or marriage, was about to crumble. The brief life of a child, premature or afflicted with a congenital disease, may so affect the nurses, doctors and aides who fight for its survival that they become "better" people because of this infant's brief existence. When Donne wrote "any man's death diminishes me, for I am involved in mankind," he didn't add "except for the deaths of premature infants who die after a few days, or hours, of life."

In the case of Alice Roe's baby—whether you believe it was stillborn or that it lived, however briefly—its life, or its existence, was certainly meaningful, more meaningful than the relatively long lives most of us lead. Its brief life (or existence) was the focus for a case that made legal history and that continues to raise moral, intellectual and legal issues that

187

may affect our lives and the lives of those born in succeeding generations. Certainly one would be hard-pressed to relate the length and meaningfulness of most lives.

Dr. Norman Virnig, the director of the newborn nurseries and newborn services at the St. Paul Ramsey Hospital in Minnesota, probably summarized the issue as well as anyone when he was asked to define viability. Here are some representative excerpts from his testimony.

It is a vast pandora's box, because a lot of people have their own definition of viability.

I would like to give you mine as best I understand it from current medical thinking, and that's that viability is the ability of the baby or the subject to exist outside the uterus.

When Flanagan asked him, "Is there any length of time involved?" Virnig answered

Yes. I want to make a clear distinction and that is that there is no real distinction as far as how long after the subject is delivered that the subject will exist outside. This is where there is disagreement among medical circles.

My own feeling is that for practical purposes there should be no time limit on viability as far as the ability to live outside the uterus.

Not a very grammatical presentation, but the meaning is clear.

Homans moved that this answer, since it admittedly represented only Virnig's opinion rather than accepted medical thinking, be stricken from the record. The judge was about to agree to strike the answer when Virnig acted to qualify it, saying in effect what we've already said—that doctors disagree

on whether a fetus should be considered viable after one day, one week or one month. The judge then let Virnig's answer stand.

In answering the defendant's appeal, the prosecution quoted from other cases—cases which had not reached the Supreme Court but dealt with the problem of manslaughter. Here is a pertinent quote from a decision by the Supreme Court of South Carolina:

> But though a human body must be alive in order that it may be the subject of homicide, yet the quantity of vitality which it retains at the moment the fatal blow is given, and the length of time life would otherwise have continued, are immaterial considerations. If any life at all is left in the human body, even the least spark, the extinguishment of it is as much homicide as the killing of the most vital being.

In summary, the prosecution said, "The law does not permit anyone to presume to measure for another what is a 'meaningful period' to survive, and the 'quality' of that survival."

The jury wouldn't have to concern itself with problems such as "viability" and "meaningful life" if they believed, as the defense wanted them to believe, that the fetus was dead when it was removed from Alice Roe's uterus, if they believed that the fetus was stillborn.

The fact that Homans brought in so many expert witnesses to testify that this baby, even if it had been born alive (as the prosecution contended) was not viable and capable of meaningful life, according to the definitions the Supreme Court intended to apply to those words, seems to me to show that he and Edelin both knew that the jury might well believe the Roe baby had indeed been born alive. They were also worried that the jury would believe Edelin might have saved the child if he

189

As Homans put it, "But we are not concerned with what the physician has to deal with after the fact, because once he commences that procedure he can't turn back. He can't say, 'Well, gee, this fetus is twenty-three and a half weeks and I thought it was twenty-two, so I am going to put it—. I don't want to be comical with this issue, it's not a comical issue, but you can see what we are getting at."

And I am sure the jury could. What Homans was saying was that, once Edelin had opened that uterus, even if he thought the fetus might be a bit older than he had anticipated, there was no way he could safely close the uterus and let Alice Roe's pregnancy continue, even had he wanted to do so. Once he opened the uterus, he was committed to removing the fetus; to do otherwise would have been contrary to reasonable surgical procedure and might well have been fatal for both Alice Roe and her child.

Nor could Edelin be held responsible for not being able to judge the fetal age as accurately as could the pathologists. Even with the uterus open, all Edelin had to use in determining fetal age were his estimates of the length and weight of the fetus. When Dr. Ward testified that in his opinion the fetus was twenty-six weeks of age, he was basing his estimate on a microscopic examination of the fetus' organs, a procedure that could only be done after the fetus was dead. It was easy, Homans in effect was saying, to second-guess a doctor when you could look at an entire case in retrospect, but that was neither a fair nor a safe procedure. A doctor simply could not function properly if he knew every step he took would later be evaluated in a courtroom where the judge, lawyers and jury had the benefit of information he couldn't possibly have had at the time he was forced to act.

But did Edelin have to act when he did? That was not touched on by either Flanagan or Homans in their summation. I believe that Edelin, or some other doctor with authority, ought to have taken a stethoscope and listened for a fetal

heartbeat on October 3, before proceeding with a hysteroto-my. If the fetus were dead—as Homans contended it might have been as a result of the failed attempts at saline abor-tion—then Alice Roe should certainly have been given the op-tion of waiting a few days for the spontaneous delivery of the baby from below. I suspect the reason no one checked for the fetal heart tones was that no one really thought the baby was dead. It may well have been that every time Edelin or anyone else put a hand on Alice Roe's abdomen, the fetus could be felt kicking and squirming around. It might well be that Edelin or someone else—a nurse perhaps—asked Alice Roe before the hysterotomy began if she still "felt life." Alice Roe might even have volunteered that information. Since Alice Roe nev-er testified, and since no one was ever asked if they had de-tected fetal movement after the failed salines and before the hysterotomy, we shall never know whether those signs of life were there. I suspect that they were. I think it is safe to con-clude that the fetus was alive and well when Edelin began the hysterotomy; and I think it's reasonable to conclude that ev-eryone associated with the case knew it.

Edelin admitted that he was not concerned with the well-being of the fetus till after it had been removed from the mother's uterus, and this is certainly amply borne out by the way he proceeded with the operation. He had not arranged to have a skilled assistant available, even though he knew or should have known that, because of the fetus' size, this was going to be a more difficult abortion by hysterotomy than he had ever seen. He made a Pfannenstiel incision, cosmetically superior to a vertical incision but more time-consuming to make and more difficult to work through. He spent extra min-utes as he operated "teaching" Steve Teich. As a result of his leisurely approach to the uterus, thirty minutes of operating time had elapsed before he was in the abdomen and ready to enter the uterus, thirty minutes during which both Alice Roe and her fetus were subjected to anesthesia—and anesthesia

invariably depresses fetal respiration. (It is less apt to be a factor in maternal respiration since the anesthetist can pump oxygen into the mother's lungs if she is so deeply anesthetized that she does not breathe adequately "on her own.")

He made a transverse incision into the uterus. Again, this takes a bit more time to make than does a vertical incision, but, in the opinion of many surgeons, it leaves the woman with a stronger scar in her uterus than does a vertical incision.

Edelin then detached the amniotic sac and placenta from the wall of the uterus. He would not have done this if he were interested in salvaging a live fetus—which, admittedly, he felt no obligation to do. He detached the placenta and the membranes because he felt that by so doing he would decrease the chance the mother would develop a postpartum infection or need a subsequent D&C to remove pieces of membrane that might otherwise be left behind.

Some doctors testified that it was acceptable procedure to detach the placenta before extracting the fetus; others testified that this was not proper procedure. Only one doctor, Dr. Alan Barnes, who was at the time of the trial a vice president of the Rockefeller Foundation in charge of medical affairs and who had previously had a long and distinguished career as an obstetrician, including professorships at Ohio State and Case Western Reserve, testified that separating the placenta before delivery would not harm the fetus. He had been called as an expert witness for the defense. Here is his testimony on cross-examination.

> Q. (**Flanagan**) If it [the fetus] remains within that particular uterus in the amniotic sac for a period of three minutes after detachment [of the placenta] would it have any means of obtaining oxygen?
> A. (**Barnes**) No, but that doesn't do it any harm.
> Q. Three minutes without oxygen would not harm it, is that correct?

194

A. That's right. May I enlarge on that?

Q. No, Doctor.

In his summation Flanagan referred briefly to Barnes' testimony (28-105):

> Well, let's get back to Dr. Barnes too. Dr. Barnes is a Rockefeller Foundation gentleman who got up here and said, "If you detach the placenta and you don't have any air for three minutes while you are in there it won't affect him." Well, I could stand here and ask you to demonstrate it by holding your breath for three minutes and see what would happen to you. Use your common sense.

I believe the jury members did use their common sense and realized that, despite Dr. Barnes testimony to the contrary, three minutes without oxygen would be damaging and possibly fatal to the fetus. (In fairness to Dr. Barnes, I suspect that if Newman Flanagan had allowed him to enlarge on his statement he would have equivocated, perhaps by saying that this particular fetus would not be damaged by anoxia since it was not a viable fetus anyway. I do not believe that Dr. Barnes really meant what he said. Being deprived of oxygen is not good for anyone. As Newman Flanagan said, "Use your common sense.")

In his summation to the jury, Bill Homans tried to discredit Giminez' testimony that Edelin stood with his hand at rest inside the uterus while staring for three minutes at a clock. Homans pointed out that (1) no one corroborated Giminez' testimony, (2) it was not even established that there were any clocks on the wall of the operating room where the hysterotomy took place and (3) Edelin would have had to turn his back on the patient and assume a very awkward position if he were to behave as Giminez said he did.

I am uncertain how to evaluate Giminez' testimony. It

195

would be nice to know if there were or were not clocks in the operating room on October 3, but since neither prosecution nor defense could establish the truth of that, I am forced to leave it as a matter for conjecture.

The awkward position that Edelin would have had to assume to watch the clock does not seem as telling to me as it apparently did to the defense. The clocks in the operating room where I generally work are on the wall toward which the patient's feet project. If I am applying pressure to, say, the oozing bed of a gallbladder which I have removed, I have to turn my head completely away from the operative site while I watch the clock. It is rather awkward, but not a movement that requires any particular gymnastic talent. And, while generally watching the clock, I can occasionally take two seconds to glance down at the gallbladder bed if I feel the need to do so. I would guess Edelin might easily have inserted his hand in the uterus, detached the placenta and amniotic sac and comfortably watched a clock on any of the operating room walls for three minutes if he chose to do so.

The most apparent weakness in Giminez' testimony is that no one else—anesthetist, operating assistant, scrub nurse or circulating nurse—would corroborate it. However, I think this weakness is more apparent than real.

After all, Giminez had nothing to do in the operating room except watch what he chose to watch. His presence was optional. He came as an observer. The anesthetist had to monitor the depth of the patient's anesthesia and check her blood pressure and other vital signs; the circulating nurse was undoubtedly bustling around checking on sponges, sutures and the other paraphernalia a surgeon needs to operate; the scrub nurse might well have been restoring order to the table on which the instruments were laid out, since that table tends to fall into disarray as an operation proceeds. I don't find it difficult at all to imagine that, if Edelin did decide to detach the contents of the uterus from the uterine wall and wait with his

hand at rest for three minutes, that that delay might have gone unnoticed by everyone but Giminez.

On the other hand, it is difficult to imagine what motive Giminez might have for claiming that Edelin stood and stared at the clock for three minutes if this were not the case. Edelin was (and is) a popular person at Boston City Hospital. Moreover, he was at the time Giminez' superior, his boss. All Giminez could possibly achieve by testifying "against" Edelin was to bring the wrath of Edelin and all his co-workers down upon his own head. But, if he did indeed observe Edelin behaving as Giminez claimed he behaved, Giminez—admittedly an antiabortionist—might well have felt a moral obligation to testify as he did.

Edelin was firm in his denial that he acted as Giminez had described. So it comes down to a question of whom do you believe: Giminez or Edelin? I suspect that what happened was this: Edelin opened the uterus and detached the amniotic sac and placenta. He then attempted to remove the sac intact with the fetus inside, but the sac ruptured almost immediately, before he had it even partly removed. Thus far, there is no disagreement; that is the sequence as Edelin described it, and Flanagan raised no questions.

Once the sac had been ruptured, Edelin could see and feel the fetus and the umbilical cord. I think that at that moment he knew with certainty what he had only suspected until that time: that the fetus was alive and the cord was pulsating. It was then, I suspect, that he looked at the clock and sent for Dr. Charles. (As you remember, he left out of his description of the operation the fact that he had sent for Dr. Charles.)

Edelin, remember, had already detached the placenta. He knew that the fetus in the uterus was not getting any oxygen from its mother. He also knew that it would die if he didn't remove it promptly; he wanted Dr. Charles' advice as to how to proceed. Waiting for Charles, he kept an eye on the clock.

Charles came into the operating room, and he and Edelin

197

discussed the situation. Charles, as director of the obstetrical service and the person ultimately responsible for what went on in the operating room, presumably told Edelin what to do. That advice might well have been "Wait till the fetus stops moving and the cord stops beating and then remove the fetus." Or, it might have been "Remove the fetus immediately and see if it's still alive." Whatever his instructions, the entire sequence, from the time Edelin opened the uterus till he finished talking with Charles, may have taken the three minutes Giminez claimed Edelin spent looking at the clock. But, while Giminez interpreted the delay as an intentional one on Edelin's part, designed to kill the fetus (and it may have been), it is also true that the three minutes might have elapsed while Edelin was getting advice as to what to do and then following that advice. Dr. Edelin says he did not intentionally delay for three minutes while watching the clock; Giminez said there was a three-minute delay while Edelin watched a clock. I believe Edelin watched the clock with his hand immobile, or relatively so, for three minutes. Part of that delay might have been intentional, but probably most of it—and possibly all—was, in Edelin's opinion, necessary. To repeat: both Edelin and Giminez told the truth as they saw the truth.

Edelin, surprisingly, was never asked either by the defense or the prosecution whether the fetus was alive when he first put his hand on it in the uterus.* I think, from what admittedly

---

*On July 12, 1977, I asked Newman Flanagan why he had not asked Edelin whether the fetus was alive *in utero.* "What do you think his answer would have been?" Flanagan asked me. "Probably that the fetus was dead," I said. "Right," Flanagan said. "So why should I ask the question? Bill Homans probably reasoned the same way; a negative reply wouldn't help and a positive answer would be devastating, so why ask?"

On August 19, 1977, Bill Homans told me, "I never even considered asking Ken that question. I doubt if he would have been cer-

went on in the OR, that there is little doubt the fetus was alive at that time. The life might have been feeble, but it was there. But the only one who will ever know whether that fetus was alive in the uterus is the one person who held that fetus in the uterus in his hand and could feel its movements, heartbeat, respirations and umbilical cord pulsations—if any. That person is, of course, Kenneth Edelin.

---

tain, even with his hand in the uterus, whether the fetus was alive or dead." I told Bill that I disagreed (and I based this opinion on my experience in performing Caesarian sections). I told him that Edelin could have known whether it was alive or dead as soon as he put his hand on the fetus. Since the question hadn't been asked of Edelin, and there was no way to resolve our difference of opinion, we dropped the matter.

19

On Friday, February 14, 1975, the twenty-ninth day of Edelin's trial, Judge McGuire gave his charge to the jury.

The charge to the jury is a summary of the legal ramifications of all that has been said and done during the trial, with a clear description of the responsibilities the jurors have in reaching a verdict, together with a delineation of the limits they must apply in arriving at a decision. Here is a pertinent excerpt from Judge McGuire's charge.

After I give you these instructions on rules of law you are required to follow them. It's not open to you to make up your own law. It's not open to you to question whether the law as I give it to you is correct or not. It's not open to you to decide that regardless of what I say about the law it ought to be different. You take the law as I give it to you. You follow it in deciding what the facts are. After deciding what the facts are, you apply to those facts the rules of law as I give them to you and render a verdict

based upon the facts as you find them to be in the law as I give it to you.

Now, you must make your decision as to what the facts of this case are solely on the basis of the evidence which was presented to you during the course of the trial, plus any valid inferences you may draw therefrom, together with a consideration of the exhibits and stipulations which counsel made as to the facts of the case.

For example, the jurors could not reach a verdict that Edelin was guilty of manslaughter if they felt that, once he had detached the placenta, he was dealing with a person. The law said that even though the fetus was detached from its mother's uterus it was not a person—and so could not be the victim of manslaughter—until it was removed, alive, from the mother's uterus.

However, it was their job to decide whether that baby had been delivered, live, from its mother's uterus. Some experts, and Edelin himself, said the baby was already dead when it was delivered. Other experts, on the basis of their microscopic examination of the lungs of the baby, had testified that the baby had breathed after removal from the uterus and so, at least by the World Health Organization definition, had been alive after removal from the uterus. It was the responsibility of the jurors to decide which of these witnesses was telling the truth. (And, as was probable, if they decided that all the witnesses were telling the truth as they saw the truth, then the jurors had the responsibility of deciding which of the witnesses were correct in their decisions.)

Later, in his instructions, Judge McGuire said:

Killing or causing the death of a person who is born alive and is outside the body of his or her mother may be the subject of manslaughter. In order for the defendant to be found guilty in this case, you must be satisfied,

202

beyond a reasonable doubt, as I have defined that term for you, that the defendant caused the death of a person who had been alive outside the body of his or her mother. If you believe beyond a reasonable doubt that the defendant, by his conduct, caused the death of a person, once that person became such as I have defined the word for you, you may find the defendant guilty of the crime of manslaughter, if that death was caused by wanton or reckless conduct on the part of the defendant. If, on the other hand, you do not find beyond a reasonable doubt that the defendant by his conduct caused the death of a person, then you must acquit him of the crime charged.

Earlier in his charge Judge McGuire had gone into the definition of manslaughter at great length. He assumed, I suppose, that the jurors would think—as I did, before I started studying this case—that manslaughter was necessarily something positive, the performance of an act, and not, possibly, the omission of an act. Here is an excerpt of instructions from Judge McGuire to the jury:

> The essence of wanton or reckless conduct is the doing of an act or the omission to act where there is a duty to act, which commission or omission involves a high degree of likelihood that substantial harm will result to another.
> Wanton or reckless conduct amounts to what has been described as indifference to or a disregard of the probable consequences to the rights of others. Wanton or reckless conduct is the legal equivalent of intentional conduct. If by wanton or reckless conduct the death is caused to another, the person guilty of such conduct may be guilty of manslaughter.

Put simply, if the Roe baby were born alive, for Edelin to

203

be guilty of manslaughter it was not necessary that he actually perform some action—put his hand over the child's mouth so that it couldn't breathe, for example—in order to be guilty of manslaughter. He was guilty of manslaughter if he acted indifferently toward the child, i.e., if he did not take positive action to help this living child keep living. By his own admission he did nothing at all to help the child after he had delivered it. So if the jurors believed the child was born alive, it would seem to follow that its subsequent death, following upon its neglect by Edelin, would necessarily make Edelin guilty of manslaughter.

It is important to note here, since it played a role in the appeal, that though Judge McGuire did not tell the jurors they could not weigh the effect of Edelin's action in detaching the placenta while the fetus was in the uterus, such instructions might have seemed implicit in his statement "In order for the defendant to be found guilty in this case, you must be satisfied, beyond a reasonable doubt, as I have defined the term for you, that the defendant caused the death of a person who had been alive outside the body of his or her mother."

There were numerous other matters on which testimony differed: the age of the fetus, the presence or absence of clocks in the operating room, Edelin's conduct in performing the hysterotomy. All these were matters of fact, not law, and it was the duty of the jurors to weigh the evidence as it had been presented to them and render a verdict. Instructions on matters of both law and fact took about two hours.

All sixteen members had remained on the jury through the fourteen days of the trial. When the judge had finished giving his charge to the jury, four names were withdrawn from the barrel and these four jurors—Frederick Spencer, Ralph Mischlen, Michael Ciano and Michael Seifort—were removed

from the jury and designated as alternate jurors to be reinstated only if one of the twelve remaining jurors became ill or, for some other reason, had to withdraw before the jury had finished its deliberations and reached a verdict.

At 12:35 P.M. the jury retired to deliberate.

The jury deliberated for seven hours before reaching a decision.

Then, at 1:20 P.M. on Saturday, February 15, 1975, the thirtieth day of the trial, the jury returned to the courtroom. The clerk asked, "Members of the jury, have you agreed on your verdict?"

The Foreman: We have, sir.

The Clerk: What say you, Mr. Foreman, on Indictment Number 81823 charging the defendant, Kenneth Edelin, with Manslaughter, is he guilty or not guilty?

The Foreman [who, according to juror Anthony Alessi, was extremely nervous and so answered very, very loudly—an action that some of the press mistakenly or maliciously attributed to a spirit of vengeance]: The defendant is guilty.

So the trial ended. Newman Flanagan asked for a delay in disposition, which was granted, and on Tuesday, February 18, 1975, Judge McGuire sentenced Kenneth Edelin to one year of probation but stayed the execution of the sentence until the final determination of his appeal. He allowed Edelin to remain free on the same bail which had been posted after the indictment.

According to juror Anthony Alessi, whose comments on the jury deliberations were published in the March 4, 1975, issue of *Harper's Weekly*, the deciding factors were (1) Dr. Ward's testimony, which the jurors believed, that the Roe

205

child had taken a breath outside its mother's uterus and (2) Edelin's conduct after the delivery of the baby. Alessi said, "We felt the doctor [Edelin] didn't give the baby enough of an opportunity. He said he placed his hand on the baby's chest for three to five seconds. We didn't weight this as a real attempt to see if the baby was alive. We took under consideration that the mother was under heavy sedation and therefore the baby was, too. With all this, well, we felt Dr. Edelin just didn't give it enough of a chance and he should have."

According to Alessi, the jurors were able to separate the manslaughter and abortion issues and to completely disregard the abortion issue. He said, "From the time we started deliberating I don't think the word 'abortion' came up twice. When it did, we all agreed that yes, there had been a legal abortion and that once the baby was detached from the mother the doctor's obligation to the mother was completed. But then we asked ourselves: did the doctor owe this baby an obligation although, granted, he was doing an abortion? And the answer we came to was yes, that under his oath as a doctor, he owed it to the baby to do more to preserve its life, since he had in his hand an individual human life separated from the mother."

Alessi said that the presence or absence of the clocks didn't seem very important to the jurors. He denied vehemently that racism played any role in their decision. The jury knew, because it was in the indictment, that the Roe baby was black but, Alessi said, "I never realized that Edelin was black until after the trial." Then he added, "And tell me this, if we were such racists [as some of the press accused them of being] and saw that it was a black baby, what the hell would we have cared? It would have been very easy for us to walk into the jury room, thrown a 'Not Guilty' into the envelope and gone home. Something held us there. When we left that room after seven hours, none of us had a reasonable doubt."

Alessi, who is a Baptist, denied that religion played any part

in the jury deliberations. He said, "As soon as we sat down, someone brought up his own religious belief, but several of us jumped up and insisted that we definitely not make religion an issue in any way."

Alessi was shocked, when the trial was over and he was able to listen to the radio and watch television and read the current newspapers as well as those published during the trial, to find out how widespread interest in the trial had been. He was also amazed to discover how bitterly many people felt about the jury's verdict. He received vicious phone calls, some from people who threatened to kill his wife and children. And he was appalled at the press coverage, which he felt was strongly biased in favor of the defense. Alessi, qualifying his comments by saying this had been his "first contact with the courts in any form," felt that both Homans and Flanagan did excellent work in presenting their cases and that Judge McGuire "handled it fairly and threated us well."

Alessi conceded that the picture of the fetus was important in their final deliberations. He said, "We passed all the evidence around the table and everyone looked at each piece, but we paid a lot of attention to that picture. None of us had ever seen a fetus before. For all we knew, a fetus looked like a kidney. The picture was obviously of a well-formed baby, over thirteen inches long. It didn't carry undue weight, but it helped us see what a baby looks like at that weight."

So, admittedly, the picture of the fetus influenced the jury, in that they now knew just what the "subject," whose death they were considering, looked like. But the effect of this single picture was hardly the element in the jury decision that columnist Harriet Van Horne claimed it was in the *Rocky Mountain News*, February 23, 1975. Ms. Van Horne said, "The jury was propelled to its verdict, in part, by the prosecution's livid display of photographs showing aborted fetal remains. Such photos are horrifying. Naturally, the pictures of doll sized embryos [sic], all in a mound, shocked the jury."

The single photo of the Roe baby which the jury was allowed to see might have been inflammatory since the case was inflammatory, but it was hardly as inflammatory as Ms. Van Horne's completely erroneous report that "pictures of doll sized embryos, all in a mound" were ever introduced as evidence.

Newman Flanagan had mailed me, at my request, a copy of the Alessi interview; *Harper's Weekly* is now defunct and the March 14 issue was not in the Minneapolis Public Library. I received a copy on July 14, 1977, and, after reading it, tried to phone Anthony Alessi, whose address is in the court record. There is no phone listed under his name.

I was, however, able to reach another juror, Liberty Ann Conlin. Ms. Conlin had been quoted in *Newsweek* (March 3, 1975) as having said, "I wish I'd had the strength to stick to my vote [not guilty]. But I was sick and tired and couldn't fight."

When I spoke to Ms. Conlin, on July 15, 1977, she told me, "At first four of us voted to find him [Edelin] not guilty. We felt sorry for him. We thought other doctors were probably doing the same thing and getting away with it.

"But the more we discussed it, the more we felt we would have to find him guilty. Just because others weren't getting caught didn't make it right to let Dr. Edelin go free.

"The picture was very important. This was a baby. You know, when you've got all these very learned men, these doctors, arguing between themselves about whether this baby was alive or not, it made it very difficult for us to decide who was right. So I'm sure the picture helped us decide that this was a baby and that Dr. Ward was right when he said it took a breath.

"Another thing influenced me," she continued. "I've had babies, and I know at six months they're alive. You can feel them kicking around. I felt Dr. Edelin, who was an obstetrician, certainly knew that, too."

208

I told her what Alessi had said about race and religion, that they hadn't played any part in the jury's verdict. "I agree completely," Ms. Conlin said. "I don't know anyone on the jury who was influenced by color or religion. I can't remember either subject coming up even once."

Finally I asked her if she agreed with Alessi that Dr. Edelin's failure to try and help the baby weighed heavily against him.

"Definitely," she said. "We didn't think he'd really tried at all to save this baby. And I knew, from having babies myself, that there was certainly some life in that baby if it was almost six months."

"You know," she said, "I'm not against abortion at all times. I think that if you've got to do one to save the life of the mother or for some other reason, then it has to be done. But you shouldn't wait till six months. If you do, then the doctor ought to try to help the baby, too."

Ms. Conlin sounded to me like a very reasonable, conscientious woman.

I suppose it is time for me to declare myself. If I had been on the jury, this, I think, is how I would have reasoned. I have purposely qualified this statement with "I think," because no one can ever know how they will behave under stress till they actually are in the stressful situation.

Dr. Kenneth Edelin began the hysterotomy on Alice Roe fully aware that the fetus in her uterus was alive. He did the hysterotomy at a leisurely pace, hoping that by the time he actually opened the uterus and amniotic sac and put his hand on the fetus, it would have died. Unfortunately for Edelin, when he got to the fetus, it was still alive. I think Edelin probably felt pulsations in the umbilical cord, a sign that the fetus' heart was beating. Such pulsations are very easily felt.

He was then uncertain as to how to proceed, so he consult-

209

ed with Dr. Charles. We do not and probably shall not know whether they decided to remove the fetus immediately or to delay another few seconds in the hope that it would die *in utero*. In either event, when he removed the fetus—now by definition, because it was outside its mother's uterus, a baby—the baby showed no signs of life. Edelin, who wanted the baby to be dead, made only a cursory search for a heartbeat and then gave the child to a nurse so she could dispose of it.

I think the Roe baby was still alive when removed from its mother's uterus; infants of twenty-two weeks' gestation are extraordinarily tough, and I doubt that three or four minutes without oxygen would have killed it. I think, if he had worked on the child, he probably could have kept it alive, though I doubt if he could have kept it alive for more than a few minutes or hours. Still, life is life and, as a doctor, I believe Edelin could and should have worked to sustain that brief life. Since he didn't, he was, in my opinion, guilty of manslaughter.

So how would I have voted? I would have voted to acquit. Because, though I think Edelin was guilty, there remains in my mind a reasonable doubt that cannot be erased, that the baby was alive when removed from the uterus; I am not as persuaded by Dr. Ward's testimony that the baby took a breath outside the uterus as were the jurors, and there was no other definite evidence that the baby was alive outside the uterus. I would have given Edelin the benefit of that reasonable doubt, as the law says I must.

I would have voted to acquit Edelin, even though I think he was guilty.

20

Edelin resumed his obstetrical practice and his work at Boston City Hospital. After his indictment on April 11, 1974, Edelin had been suspended from the staff of Boston City Hospital, but the protests both by the medical and lay people of Boston had been so vehement that his suspension had been lifted a week later. From that time until it was necessary to devote all his days to his trial, Edelin had not only continued to practice obstetrics and to work at Boston City Hospital but had also spoken at numerous meetings in cities all across the country. He had become a symbol around which the proabortionists rallied.

I know nothing of Kenneth Edelin's income before, during or after his trial, but I was told by one of his close associates that "Ken certainly hasn't suffered financially. In fact, there isn't any doubt that all this publicity has helped him increase his income enormously." Certainly, as Bill Homans had told me, there was plenty of money flowing into the Kenneth Edelin defense fund.

211

William A. Nolen, M.D.

On April 5, 1976, Homans filed an appeal before the Supreme Court of Massachusetts. In it he reviewed all the arguments he had advanced at the time of the trial, and there is little point in a detailed review of the appeal. Nor would any point be served by summarizing the commonwealth's answer to the appeal or the defendant's reply to the commonwealth's answer. Basically, the defense thought Judge McGuire should have moved for a directed verdict of acquittal, since the prosecution had failed to prove its case. They also felt that the judge had given the jury far more responsibility than they should have had—that if Judge McGuire had spelled out the matters of law in greater detail, then the jury would have arrived at a "not guilty" verdict.

Flanagan, arguing for the prosecution, felt that not only were the judge's instructions clear and proper but that the jury had acted wisely in returning the verdict of "guilty."

Ordinarily there are seven judges on the Supreme Court, but on this case one judge disqualified himself, reportedly because he had discussed the Edelin case with Bill Homans before he—the judge—had been appointed to the bench.

It was expected that the Supreme Court would deliver its decision in the early fall of 1976, but as October and November came and went without any word from the court, Homans became increasingly concerned. "The problem," he told me, when I visited with him on December 15, 1976, "is that, with six judges, if we wind up with a three-three tie, the verdict stands as it is. I expected it to be close, but I think that on at least one of the grounds of our appeal we would win, if there were seven judges sitting. As it is, the longer they delay, the more worried I become."

The prosecution seemed to me much more confident. I had lunch with two lawyers who were associated with the district attorney's office, and they admitted they felt their case would stand up to the appeal. "It should," one of them said. "Newman did a fine job in arguing the case, and he had the evi-

dence. As he told you, he wouldn't have gone to court if he didn't think he could win. No one needs the kind of trouble this case has given us.''

Homans was also chagrined about losing one of the jurors whose name had been taken from the barrel before deliberations had begun. "In most states they drop the last jurors selected,'' he said, "so this fellow, having been selected early, would have been in on the final deliberations. And he has told me, and the press, that nothing would have persuaded him to vote for conviction. But that's the way things go. Just bad luck.''

Even now, though he was obviously worried about the outcome, Homans remained even-tempered and philosophical. If there is one word that I would never think of applying to Bill Homans, that word is "bitter.'' He has had his share of knocks, both in and out of the courtroom, but he retains his composure and good humor.

On December 17, less than an hour after I had met Edelin and interviewed Dr. Ed Lowe at Boston City Hospital, the Supreme Court announced its verdict. They reversed the manslaughter conviction of Dr. Kenneth Edelin. Five of the six justices voted to clear him completely, which meant he would not have to go through a new trial. Chief Justice Edward F. Hennesey agreed the conviction should be set aside but felt Edelin should be tried again.

All the judges felt there was insufficient evidence to find Edelin guilty of wanton reckless conduct that caused the death of the male child, as the indictment had alleged. They felt that even though later tests showed the child might have been fleetingly alive, since those tests were not available to Edelin at the time of the hysterotomy, and since he had apparently made a good faith judgment that the child was dead when delivered, he should not be found guilty of wanton misconduct.

The decision was, however, closer than was superficially

213

apparent, since two of the judges (Justices Reardon and Quirico) supported reversal of conviction only because in their view Judge McGuire's instructions at the trial limited the jurors to considering only the actions Edelin took after completing the abortion. Feeling as they did, they might well have voted along with Chief Justice Hennesey for a new trial rather than reversal of the conviction, in which case a new trial would have been held. I suspect they voted for reversal to spare everyone the agonies of a new trial.

On July 12, 1977, I phoned Newman Flanagan and asked him what the judges had had to say about Judge McGuire's instructions to the jury. "Nothing," Newman said. "They just pointed out that, according to Judge McGuire's instructions, the jurors couldn't consider anything Edelin did prior to delivery of the baby."

Under the common law that was in force in Massachusetts at the time of the Roe abortion, the jury should have been allowed to consider Edelin's conduct prior to removal of the baby. The law said that if an action were taken prior to delivery of a baby and that action resulted in injury to that fetus *in utero*, and if the baby was then born alive and died shortly thereafter of injuries received *in utero* then the person who had caused the injury was guilty of murder or manslaughter. Edelin's detachment of the placenta, the prosecution had contended, was an *in-utero* blow to the baby, and the jury should have considered the role it played in the eventual death of the baby after it had been born alive. But, since two of the Supreme Court justices believed that Judge McGuire's instructions forbade the jurors from considering the actions Edelin had taken while the child was *in utero*, then, they felt, the jurors could not reasonably find Edelin guilty.

Another factor in the Edelin reversal—the factor which Bill Homans thought had most influenced the Massachusetts judges—was a decision the United States Supreme Court had handed down on July 6, 1976, after the Edelin appeal had been

filed but before it had been decided. The case, *Danforth* (the attorney general of Missouri, appellant) v. *Planned Parenthood of Central Missouri*, was concerned with certain restrictions the state of Missouri had chosen to apply to abortions. In the Supreme Court's decision they said, among other things:

> In "Roe," we used the term "viable," properly we thought, to signify the point at which the fetus is potentially able to live outside the mother's womb, albeit with artificial aid, and presumably capable of "meaningful life outside the mother's womb." We noted that this point is usually placed "at about seven months or twenty-eight weeks, but may occur earlier."

Now the Supreme Court, in *Danforth* v. *Planned Parenthood of Central Missouri*, added:

> "In any event, we agree with the District Court that it is not the proper function of the legislature or the courts to place viability, which essentially is a medical concept, at a specific point in the gestation period. The time when viability is achieved may vary with each pregnancy, and the determination of whether a particular fetus is viable is, and must be, a matter for the judgment of the responsible attending physician.

Homans made a copy of this decision for me, as we talked in his office a day before the Massachusetts Supreme Court reversed the Edelin conviction. "In the face of this decision by the Supreme Court," Homans said, "I don't think they ought to let Ken's conviction stick. But you never know."

Since in their reversal the Massachusetts Supreme Court referred to the U.S. Supreme Court's decision of July 6, including the portion which said "the determination of whether

215

a particular fetus is viable is, and must be, a matter for the judgment of the responsible attending physician," it is apparent that Homans was correct: the Danforth decision did influence the Massachusetts Supreme Court. The question remains, however, as to how great a role the Danforth decision played in the Massachusetts case. The weight each justice gave to each factor is simply not measurable.

So the trial really ended much as it had begun: in a muddle. Edelin was declared not guilty but, much as the proabortionists wanted to read into his acquittal some widely applicable rule that could be applied to other cases and to abortion in general, no such interpretation was even remotely possible. Conviction was based to a large extent on a technicality and applied only to this specific case.

In their conclusion the judges stated this very specifically:

This opinion does not seek an answer to the question when abortions are morally justifiable and when not. That question is wholly beyond our province. Rather we have dealt with a question of guilt or innocence under a particular statute on a particular state of facts.

Problems related to abortion are as far from resolution in 1978 as they were when the Supreme Court's decision in *Roe* v. *Wade* became the law of the land in January 1973.

21

The trial was, as might be expected, a major story in Boston and was extensively covered by the media—press, television and radio.

The news reporting and even more emphatically the editorial comment were sympathetic to Edelin. Supporters of the prosecution felt the reporting was more than sympathetic, that it was strongly slanted in support of Edelin.

I was not in Boston while the trial was going on so I did not personally watch the television coverage, listen to the radio or read the two major newspapers—the *Globe* and the *Herald*—as the trial progressed. However, even those who supported Edelin have told me that they were well satisfied with the press coverage. "He deserved support," several of the pro-Edelin faction said, "and he got it."

Those who felt, as the trial progressed, that Edelin was guilty felt that the media weighted their reporting of the trial strongly in favor of the defense. "I went to the trial a few times," a Right-to-Life advocate told me, "and then at night

William A. Nolen, M.D.

I'd watch the television reports and the next day I'd read the papers. I could hardly believe the reporters were at the same trial I attended. They'd leave out anything that tended to discredit the defense and emphasize every minor slip the prosecution might make. It's a good thing the jurors weren't allowed to listen to television or radio reports or read the papers. If they had, I think they'd have been scared to vote for conviction even if they felt Edelin was guilty. They'd have been afraid their neighbors would be ready to lynch them when the trial was over."

One person who was herself a supporter of Edelin told me, "There's no question in my mind; the media went all out for Ken. I'm glad, of course, but I'm willing to admit the papers, television and radio did give the prosecution an awfully hard time. I'd have to agree that they were often vicious in their treatment of Newman Flanagan, and he didn't deserve it. He's a decent man who had a difficult job to do, and he did it fairly and very well. I felt sorry for him."

After the trial, I did read some of the editorial comments in the press and I'd have to agree: most, but not all, the reporters and columnists were pro-Edelin. David O'Brian's column in the *Boston Herald* in early 1977 both reflects and comments on the press coverage of the trial. In a column entitled IS JURY SYSTEM A GAME OF CHANCE? he says, "Such doubts [concerning the jury system] began to concern me early in 1975 when—despite a pointed charge from Judge James McGuire which reporters covering the trial in question interpreted as a virtual mandate for an innocent verdict—a Suffolk County jury found Dr. Kenneth Edelin guilty of manslaughter for performing what even the prosecution conceded was a perfectly legal and proper abortion.

"That outrageous finding has now been overturned by the State Supreme Court which found, indeed, that said jury simply did not reach the obvious conclusion to which the weight of evidence should have taken it; that Dr. Edelin acted totally

218

in accordance with accepted medical practice and never should have been dragged into a courtroom in the first place."

Anthony LaCamera, another columnist for the *Boston Herald*, gave his opinion of the press coverage in an article called "Fairness and the Edelin Case," which was published weeks after Edelin's conviction. Here are representative excerpts:

Like it or not, there is a sizeable backlash hereabouts to the allegedly one-sided manner in which certain elements of the broadcast media handled the aftermath of the Dr. Kenneth C. Edelin manslaughter verdict. . . .

With some justification, the feeling in sometimes ignored quarters is that it has been open season on the Irish-American sector of our community—or, more specifically, on Irish Catholics. . . .

Certain television and radio personalities involved in the media coverage of the extremely complex Edelin situation did not report or even moderate. They seemed far more interested in selling whether through their overall attitude or through neat little one-sentence observations. Emotion-charged comments aimed against the Edelin jury members (who, ironically, were accused of emotionalism) came darned close to being inflammatory.

LaCamera then went on to quote from a woman who had responded with a letter to what she considered a biased, pro-Edelin television show. "I never thought that I'd see the day when 'pro-life' would take on a negative meaning and that anyone who was opposed to the unnecessary taking of human life would be looked upon as someone who needed enlightening. Somewhere the table of values has turned." (Subsequently, the criticized television show devoted a program to an expression of the pro-life group's sentiments.)

To understand the media bias, it's important to remember that as the trial progressed, the busing controversy in Boston

219

was also at its peak. Every day young black children were being stoned by whites when they were bussed from their neighborhoods to all-white schools. It was natural to feel revulsion at the treatment blacks in general were receiving in Boston; reading of the busing controversy, far removed from it all in Minnesota, I felt nothing but loathing for the crowds that beat up the black youngsters. It's easy to understand how the press could be swayed, consciously or unconsciously, to Edelin's support—to make him, even against his will, a martyr in the cause of justice for the blacks.

Bias in the media is sometimes difficult if not impossible to avoid. But—as most reporters would agree—it should never be condoned. (Even as I write this I know I, too, will be accused of bias. I anticipate the accusation and can only say I am doing my very best to report the Edelin case objectively.)

Network radio and television coverage was not extensive, but many national magazines published articles on the case. *Newsweek*, in its issue of March 5, 1975, featured an article on the Edelin case and abortion in general and even ran a picture of a sixteen-week-old fetus on its cover.

I read most of the magazine articles that dealt with the case, and it seemed to me that they showed a definite pro-Edelin slant.

An exception, as might be expected, was William Buckley's conservative *National Review*. Here is one of the final paragraphs from an article that appeared in the issue of March 14, 1975.

One must ask, why Edelin? On the face of it, he is a dubious hero for the Champions of permissive abortion. He killed a well-formed child, whether with technical legality being a secondary point. Prudence would seem to recommend that the pro-abortionists keep a discreet distance from such a case, and take refuge in the usual

220

banalities about the 'complexities' and 'sensitivity' of the issue. But Edelin, like his client and his victim, is a Negro. The case can be presented as the lynching of a black Marcus Welby by a bigoted community.

Franz Ingelfinger, M.D., then the editor (as of 1977 the editor emeritus) of the prestigious *New England Journal of Medicine*, evoked the wrath of many physicians when, shortly after Edelin's conviction, he published a strong pro-Edelin editorial entitled, "The Edelin Trial Fiasco." He opened his article with a quote from the *Washington Post*, which said, "By convicting Dr. Kenneth Edelin for manslaughter, the state of Massachusetts has brought disgrace to itself and the whole judicial system. The charge against the doctor should never have been brought by the prosecutor. The trial judge should never have allowed the case to go to the jury. And the jury's verdict itself is suspect."

Dr. Ingelfinger made it clear that he agreed with the *Post*'s view of the case. Later in his editorial he said, "The Edelin Case is a fiasco. As Dr. Kenneth Ryan has said, 'This court trial on abortion has not established the fundamental facts on viability, has not established what an abortion is, and certainly has not established the moral issues any more than the Scopes Trial was the last word on evolution. In addition, the trial has hardened the positions, inflamed the rhetoric, and disrupted rational exchange between the pro-abortionists and anti-abortionists."

Ingelfinger ended his editorial with this paragraph: "Individuals who believe that the trial has been a complete failure in settling anything and that, at the same time, it abrogated Dr. Edelin's right to a normal life, will wish to support his appeal to higher court. Contributions may be sent to the Kenneth Edelin Defense Fund, Suite 302, 15 Broad Street, Boston, MA 02109." It was this appeal for funds that particu-

221

so do women who are unmarried and, because they forgot to use a contraceptive (or the contraceptive failed, as contraceptives sometimes do), find themselves pregnant and feel they are either incapable of raising a child as a single parent or are convinced that to do so is unfair to the child.

Unwanted pregnancies are not uncommon now, but they were far more common twenty-five years ago when contraceptive methods were crude in comparison to what is available in 1977 and contraceptive information was difficult, if not impossible, to obtain. I felt sorry for those women twenty-five years ago—many of whom were friends or wives of friends—and I feel sorry for these women today. I only wish—as I'm sure that women then and women now do—that unwanted pregnancies never occurred. I also wish, as again, I'm sure they do, that abortion might never have to be utilized as the solution to an unwanted pregnancy. But human nature being what it is—and as the father of six living children, with a wife who has not only borne these six children but also suffered through two miscarriages and given birth to a seventh child who lived only an hour, I am fully cognizant of the temptations of the flesh that are part of human nature—I realize that unwanted pregnancies are going to occur. And I agree that, for those who choose abortion (probably with reluctance) as the answer to that unwanted pregnancy, abortion should be safely, conveniently, inexpensively available.

But I also know that—except in those rare instances such as rape or pregnancy in a mentally deficient person—the person who gets pregnant is responsible to some degree for that pregnancy. In some early civilizations the fact that pregnancy resulted from intercourse was not known; after all, nine months routinely elapsed between the two events, and the cause and effect relationship was not immediately clear. But the relationship between the two—with very few exceptions—is now general knowledge. When we indulge in intercourse, we know that pregnancy may result (assuming, of course, that neither

party has been sterilized). Which means, of course, that in virtually all pregnancies women (and men) must logically assume some responsibility for the existence of that pregnancy.

So, I agree, the woman who wants an unwanted pregnancy terminated should have that right. Nor would I presume to classify the motive for her choice as good, bad or indifferent. No one can know another person well enough to make that judgment.

Obviously, abortion has—despite the protestations of the antiabortionists—achieved not only legal but moral acceptance, and not only in the United States but in most other countries of the world. The United States rate of abortion is twenty-two per thousand women of reproductive age. In Denmark the comparable figure is twenty-seven; in East Germany, twenty-nine; Finland, twenty-one; Norway, twenty; Sweden, twenty; England, eleven; Canada, ten; and Scotland, eight.

In view of these figures it is futile to argue that abortion is no longer acceptable, at least under some circumstances, to a large segment of the population. It is, however, possible to argue that abortion is immoral. That argument, as we are all aware, has vigorous, vociferous support. While doing the research for and writing of this book, I sought, as I said in my preface, to learn all I could from the Edelin trial in the hope that I might then be able to make some helpful suggestions as to how our society might best cope with the problem of abortion. This I shall now attempt to do.

First, let me say that to a doctor—certainly, to this doctor—abortion seems a mockery of all of the other things I do in my work. Much of my time—most of my working hours—are devoted to trying as best I can to keep people alive. Abortion, rationalize the procedure as you may, is an act in which the doctor terminates a potential life.

And not only does he (or she; I use "he" to stand for doctors since the majority of doctors in this country are still male)

225

terminate the life or the potential life of an infant (or fetus or baby) but he is terminating (terminate is an euphemism for kill or destroy) a life which, in 1978, may be expected to last, on an average, 72.8 years.

On the other hand, the lives we physicians struggle to save are, with growing frequency as the average age of our population increases, those of people already in their 70s or 80s who have at most a life expectancy of ten or fifteen years. It would seem reasonable that what we ought to do is let die the 70- and 80-year-old people who, assuming they survive our operations, medications and X-ray treatments, will probably have to settle for less than optimum health. It is very expensive to keep them alive. On the other hand, to keep a twenty-week-old fetus alive so that in another eighteen weeks it will emerge from its mother's womb, presumably hale and hearty, ready to enjoy a long healthy, happy life, is not an arduous or expensive task. All we have to do is do nothing. Nature will do the job for us.

I am being a little bit facetious but not entirely so. Perhaps my suggestion will seem less unrealistic if I put it another way. Our society has a limited amount of money to spend on health care. Assume I have as a patient an eighty-year-old woman with extensive cancer whose life I can prolong for several months only by performing an expensive operation. (About one-fourth of the expense will be my fee; the other three-quarters will be hospital charges.) I have another patient, a pregnant woman, who needs a Caesarian section so that her fetus can become a baby. In this hypothetical case there is money (or hospital equipment or medical staff) sufficient to treat only one of these patients. Which patient should we treat? I think we would find few people who would say, "Treat the eighty-year-old woman"; I would expect that even the eighty-year-old woman might say, "Go ahead and save the infant's life. Let me die." With medical expenses increas-

226

ing rapidly, and likely to continue to do so, we may be forced to make choices not unlike this hypothetical one in the near future. In fact, in deciding which recipients will receive available donor kidneys, we are already choosing which patients we will save and which we will let die.

Now, admittedly, when we perform abortions we are dealing with unwanted babies, if we define "unwanted" in terms of the mother. In all probability, since there are currently long lists of people waiting to adopt babies, the baby would be "wanted" by someone. But perhaps, since the baby is unwanted by its mother, it does not deserve the care and attention a wanted baby would get; perhaps, since it is unwanted, it is proper to destroy it. This is the position you must defend if you are in favor of granting women a virtually unrestricted right to have an abortion.

But let us not pretend to ourselves that that is what the unwanted baby wants. I know, personally, hundreds of children and adults who were, before their births, unwanted. (For all I know, I may fall into that category; I've never asked my mother if I was wanted or unwanted and I don't intend to ask her. Nor do I want any of our six children to ask that question of Joan and me.) Most of these unwanted children are now "wanted" by their parents. And even the few who may still be "unwanted" don't show any great desire to oblige their parents by committing suicide. Given a choice, they, like most human beings, prefer life to death. The "unwanted" hang on to life as tenaciously as do the "wanted."

We may as well also make it clear now that all this nonsense about "unwanted" babies ending up as "battered children" is just that: nonsense. I have never seen any figures to demonstrate conclusively that even a minimal correlation exists. Wanted children are battered by their parents with approximately the same frequency as unwanted children. Children are battered by a parent because the parent is permanently or

temporarily deranged. The derangement has nothing to do with whether the child was, before birth, wanted or unwanted.

Dr. Ira S. Lourie, coordinator of child abuse programs for the National Institute of Mental Health, told me, "We are in an era where the incidence of reporting of child abuse is skyrocketing. There are so many factors that contribute to child abuse that statistics that show any reduction in the incidence of child abuse due to liberalization of the abortion laws are simply not available."

Dr. Michael Bazerman, associate professor at the University of Minnesota's Center for Youth Development and Research, put it another way. "People who really know about child abuse," he said, "would never get caught saying 'the unwanted child is more likely to be battered than is the wanted child.' The whole problem of child abuse is far too complicated for such generalizations."

Dr. Robert tenBencel, professor of pediatrics and director of the Department of Maternal and Child Health at the University of Minnesota Medical School, told me, "Actually, there are some studies which show that it's the child who is most wanted who is most likely to be battered by the parents. These studies show, for example, that among battered children there is a high incidence of children who are named after their parents and that the mothers of battered children tended to wear maternity clothes earlier than the average mother because they were so pleased to be pregnant.

"What happens, of course, is that the parents have unrealistic expectations with which they burden their children, and when the children don't live up to expectations, they are battered.

"There's certainly no evidence that liberalized abortion laws have resulted in a decrease in the number of battered children. It may well be that just the opposite is true."

228

As Dr. Joseph Stanton had testified at Dapper O'Neil's hearing, the incidence of child abuse in New York "soared" after the introduction of liberal abortion policies in 1972. (Though, in fairness to the proabortion group, the increased incidence of child abuse is probably not due to the liberalized abortion policy as much as it is to our increased awareness and reporting of such cases.)

However, clearly—and this is the point—liberalized abortion policies have not reduced the number of cases of child abuse. The obstetricians who advance as an argument in favor of abortion the theory that the unwanted child will probably become a battered child do not have a statistical leg to stand on.

Lest I be thought of as a rigid conservative, let me, before we get deeper into my suggestions regarding a proper approach to abortion, quote two paragraphs from a journal which is universally and deservedly classified as liberal and which has been and is a staunch defender of the rights of women to have abortions as they please—within, of course, the limits stipulated by the Supreme Court in *Roe* v. *Wade*. These paragraphs are from an editorial in the July 2, 1977, issue of *The New Republic*, an editorial provoked by the Supreme Court's decision that states did not have to provide funds for indigent women who wanted elective abortions.

'Roe v. Wade' killed off the movement for abortion reform, by making it seem superfluous. But this was the moment life began—conception, "quickening," viability, birth: Choose your own metaphor—for the right to life movement. In four years it has become one of the most powerful political lobbies in the country. The power is based not on numbers but on passion. It is inspiring, in a way. Since the end of the antiwar movement, these misguided [sic] people represent the only major pressure

229

group on the political scene whose cause is not essentially self-interest. They speak for what is in their minds a
truly unrepresented minority: fetuses.

I have called attention to the word "misguided" because I
think that word makes explicit the fact that *The New Republic*
is unquestionably proabortion. Even though an editorial is, by
definition, an expression of opinion, it seems to me that for
modesty's sake, if for no other reason, the author of the editorial might have qualified "misguided" by inserting "in our
opinion," either before or after the word.

However, the paragraph from the same editorial which I
thought most interesting, with which I agree wholeheartedly
and which I expect proabortionists are going to find very difficult to swallow, is this:

> Those who believe a woman should be free to have an
> abortion must face the consequences of their beliefs.
> Metaphysical arguments about the beginning of life are
> fruitless. But there clearly is no logical or moral distinc-
> tion between a fetus and a young baby; free availability
> of abortion cannot be reasonably distinguished from eu-
> thanasia. Nevertheless we are for it. It is too facile to say
> that human life always is sacred; obviously it is not, and
> the social cost of preserving against the mother's will the
> lives of fetuses who are not yet self-conscious is simply
> too great.

When I read that paragraph I wanted to stand up and cheer.
At last someone—a proabortion, liberal someone—had said
what needed to be said. We have an obligation to stop playing
games, hiding behind euphemisms, arguing over shades of
meaning of the word "viability" and face a very distasteful
fact: when we perform an abortion, we are destroying a life.
We may choose to do that—some of us do choose to do it—

230

but abortion is murder and there is no way we can, if we are honest, deny that revolting fact. (I do have one quibble with the paragraph I applaud. *The New Republic* refers to fetuses as "not yet self-conscious." To make that claim is, I think, an example of the kind of rationalizing that *The New Republic* advises us to avoid. On what grounds does *The New Republic* say that fetuses are not "self-conscious"? A sixteen-week-old fetus will kick and squirm if prodded by a needle. That, it would seem to me, is very simple evidence that the fetus is self-conscious. Perhaps a sixteen-week-old fetus does not spend time, as it bobs around in the amniotic sac, thinking about the meaning of life or musing on the works of Plato, but neither does a two-year-old toddler.

Dr. Fernando Torres, an expert in the field of electroencephalography, told me, "The electroencephalogram of a twenty-week-old fetus is virtually identical with that of a newborn infant, except that in the twenty-week-old fetus there are periods of inactivity which alternate with the periods of activity." This certainly suggests that a twenty-week-old fetus and a newborn are about equally self-conscious.

But insisting that abortion is murder (not legally, perhaps, but morally) does not really change things, as the statistics I quoted earlier show. Abortion is unquestionably acceptable to many if not most human beings. According to that previously quoted editorial in *The New Republic*, the percentage of Americans who favor abortion on demand runs, depending on which polls you accept, somewhere between 67 and 81 percent.

As I worked on this book I also took a poll—admittedly not a "scientific" one in the sense that the Roper and Gallup polls are scientific, but one which I found informative. I think my poll added something to the cold statistics that result from formal polling.

I discussed the matter of abortion with a lot of men and women of various ages. Some were strong antiabortionists;

231

others felt that a woman had the right to determine what, if anything, should be done to the fetus she was carrying, right up till the moment before it was delivered. One woman and her husband—and I'll admit this is an extreme example—actually felt strongly that, until the child was seven years old, the traditional age of reason, the parents had the right to kill the child if they so wished.

What I found most intriguing, however, was that almost invariably, when I got away from generalities and started asking about specific cases, the differences in opinion between the pro- and antiabortionists became much less clear, much more poorly defined than initially seemed the case.

For example, when I would ask a strong antiabortionist how she would feel if the woman we were considering had been raped by her father and the child she was carrying was known to be—through studies done on the amniotic fluid—suffering from severe mental retardation, many of the antiabortion women would say, "Well, in that case I guess I'd make an exception." And, almost without exception, an antiabortion man would say, "In that sort of instance there is no question in my mind. Abortion would be the proper choice."

At the other extreme, when I'd ask a strong proabortion woman how she would feel if the pregnant girl were twenty years old, had been impregnated by an intelligent young man with whom she had been carrying on an affair and had allowed the pregnancy to progress to twenty-six weeks so that for ten weeks what was, as far as could be determined, a healthy young fetus-infant had been kicking around inside the mother, the proabortion woman would say, "Well, since she's let things go so long, I guess I'd recommend she have the baby and put it up for adoption." Proabortion men would express similar views.

It was clear that in specific cases, differences were more apparent than real. Sure, there were a few radical antiabortion-

ists who felt that a twelve-year-old carrying a retarded child, the result of rape by her father, should not be given the option of an abortion; and a few rabid proabortionists felt it was all right to abort at eight months a healthy, thriving fetus, the product of conception of two willing, intelligent individuals; but very few people fell into these extremist groups. And I had the feeling that in most instances if the cases I was presenting were real, not hypothetical, both the pro- and anti-abortionists would have given ground and reached, what seemed to most of those I questioned, a reasonable decision.

In my informal poll I thought of asking the parents of defective children—parents whose children were mongoloids, had progressive muscular dystrophy or myelomeningocoeles which made them incontinent and/or mentally retarded—if, assuming they had been offered the choice, they would have chosen to have abortions rather than give birth to these children; but I couldn't bring myself to ask the question. It seemed too cruel.

Besides, I didn't think I could get an honest answer from them. I doubted that even they knew what choice they might have made. Of one thing I was certain, since a number of parents of defective children are friends or patients of mine and I know them well: without exception the parents lavish love and affection on their deformed children. It is almost a cliché to say that having a deformed child unites parents more closely than almost any other tragedy. Like most clichés, this one is true.

However, I was not reluctant to ask friends and patients a theoretical question: if they learned before the twentieth week of pregnancy, through studies on the amniotic fluid, that the child to be born in another eighteen weeks would be severely retarded, mentally and/or physically, would they elect to have an abortion? Fifty percent of the wives and 75 percent of the husbands said they thought they would choose to have

233

an abortion, though they admitted they could not say with certainty how they would behave unless they actually found themselves in that predicament.

The religion of those I questioned didn't seem to be a critical factor. I had expected it would. The Catholics answēred my questions—when I asked them to consider admittedly extreme cases—as did Protestants, Jews and agnostics. When we dealt with the less extreme cases, the religious differences and the philosophical pro- or antiabortion differences became more apparent. For example, a proabortionist (better called a pro woman's-right advocate) would condone abortion for a seventeen-year-old high school senior pregnant as the result of a casual affair with a classmate; an antiabortionist, which included most Catholics, would oppose the right of the woman to an abortion under such circumstances.

There were also differences of opinion which depended on the age of the patient interviewed. Women and men in their late teens and early twenties had a much more casual attitude about abortion than did women over forty. Put simply, younger people didn't consider abortion as radical a solution to an unwanted pregnancy as did older people.

With one exception. Once I started asking about abortion after sixteen weeks, the age at which the fetus begins to kick and move and the mother can "feel life," all men and women felt that the grounds for abortion should be much more stringent than at earlier stages of pregnancy. Men and women of all ages would invariably ask, "Why didn't she [the mother] do something earlier? If she didn't want to have a child, then she certainly should have been able to make her mind up in less than four months." Even the strong proabortionists, though they might go along with the woman's right to an abortion at any stage of pregnancy, would become angry at a pregnant woman who would let a pregnancy proceed past the sixteenth week. (This condemnation was not extended to the

twelve-year-old and/or mentally retarded girl who didn't realize she was pregnant till the pregnancy was far advanced.)

The conclusions of the extensive but informal poll that I took as I wrote this book were as follows:

(1) The differences between the pro- and antiabortion public tend to disappear when extreme cases are under consideration.

(2) Young women and men (under forty, roughly) are apt to consider abortion a less radical answer to an unwanted pregnancy than are older men and women.

(3) Both the pro- and antiabortion groups felt that, whenever possible—which is the case at least 90 to 95 percent of the time—a woman ought to make a decision for or against abortion before the pregnancy reaches five months.

(4) Both pro- and antiabortionists agreed that the ideal solution to the abortion problem would be wider dissemination of information about and the means to practice birth control, provided some method could also be found to persuade people to use this information and equipment. Unfortunately there is little hope that this will be achieved. According to Planned Parenthood, 80 percent of sexually active teen-agers reported that they had intercourse at some time without birth control. Fifty percent hadn't used contraceptives the last time they'd had intercourse. The information and the means presumably available to most of these teen-agers are worthless when they are not willing to use them.

(5) When I asked couples what they would do if they learned, at the sixteenth week of pregnancy, that the fetus in its mother's uterus would be born mentally retarded, about half said they would have an abortion, the others said they would have the child.

Admittedly, once a child is born, handicapped though he or she may be, the parents become emotionally attached to the child; we rarely read of a handicapped child being battered by

235

its parents. This after-the-fact question must be considered in a special light. Its chief significance is, I think, that it demonstrates quite clearly that we can't predict how we will feel or react to certain events until they have occurred—a point I will soon discuss further.

Essentially, where our questions overlapped, my informal poll yielded the same results as the formal poll the defense conducted before the trial. (In that poll the question was asked "Do you believe it is *right* for a doctor to perform an abortion on a pregnant woman in at least *some* cases, such as where having the baby might *endanger* the mother's life, or do you believe it is *always wrong* for a doctor to perform an abortion?" Of all the prospective jurors questioned [56 percent of whom were Catholic] a minimum of 72 percent and a maximum of 97 percent [depending on how the jurors were subdivided: by race, religion, income, etc.] answered "Right in at least some cases." Over all, about 80 percent condoned abortion for at least some cases.)

23

Obviously, there isn't any one solution to the problem of abortion—certainly not one which will be acceptable to the extremists in either the pro-or antiabortion group.

We may as well agree to disagree. Some of us are going to accept abortion as an answer to an unwanted pregnancy; others of us are not. Personally, I don't intend to perform any abortions; I find the idea repellent.

I think it is safe to say (though exact figures are not available) that my feelings regarding abortion are more the rule than the exception among physicians.

The Supreme Court did not, in *Roe* v. *Wade,* insist that all hospitals and all doctors perform abortions; it simply made abortions legal. The physicians in about 80 percent of the hospitals in the United States do not permit members of the staff to perform abortions in the hospital. In all of South Dakota there is not one hospital where physicians are allowed to perform abortions. The prohibition of abortion is, generally, a

decision made by the medical staff and customarily reflects the wishes of the majority of the people the hospital serves.

In South Dakota (I refer to this state only because the information is available; in other states there is no record of how many doctors will perform abortions in their offices or in hospitals) there is only one doctor who admits he performs abortions. And as I write this (August 1977) he is being threatened with a manslaughter charge because of the death of a woman which resulted from an abortion performed in 1973.

Again, I am not criticizing those physicians whose consciences allow or even compel them to perform abortions. I am saying that such physicians are, in all probability, a minority of the total physician pool.

This does not mean, however, that I feel I have either an obligation or a right to criticize all doctors who perform abortions. If their consciences will allow them—or possibly even compel them—to use their skills to perform abortions for women who want or need them, that is their privilege. In fact, I will probably do as I have done in the past—refer to such doctors those women who want abortions and whom I prefer not to treat. These doctors will do what I consider dirty work for me. It is not my place to criticize them.

Nor do I want to be accused of having a holier-than-thou attitude toward physicians who will perform abortions, though I will probably be so accused. My reluctance to perform abortions stems, I suppose, from several causes: my Irish-Catholic heritage (though I am not much of a practicing Catholic); my age (fifty) and the traditions that are part of my generation; and my medical training, which took place between 1949 and 1960, when abortions were illegal. Younger doctors, I expect, like younger people in general, may find abortions less repellent than do I.

I do not consider myself inflexible. When I came to Litchfield in 1960, I wouldn't perform sterilizations, nor would many of the other doctors on our staff. Now I do perform

them. But I've drawn a line this side of abortions; I don't plan to step over it. I neither brag about nor apologize for my position on abortions.

I think, however, that a note of caution should be sounded. The woman who elects to have an abortion must realize that once it is done it cannot be undone, that she is going to have to live with the consequences of that decision for the rest of her life. Admittedly some women are very happy after having had an abortion. For most of them this happiness continues; they never have a regret, at least as long as doctors have so far been able to study them.

But other women, months or even years after having had an abortion, are plagued with recurring bouts of remorse. They feel guilty about the life which they chose to have terminated. Even Alice Roe, a few months after the Edelin case had ended, told one of her close friends, "If I had it to do again, I think I might not have had that abortion. I would certainly have given one of the alternatives more serious consideration." At that time she was four years older, a student in a university and, perhaps, a wiser girl than she had been at seventeen when she had chosen to have an abortion.

Dr. Hugh Holtrop, who played an important role in the Edelin case and who had agreed that abortion was the proper choice for Alice Roe, told me of his experience with teen-age girls who have abortions. "I don't have exact figures," he said, "but I have been very impressed with a rather bizarre phenomenon. Many of these fifteen- and sixteen-year-old girls who have abortions come back just a few months later, pregnant again, only this second time around they have and keep the baby. They feel guilty after their first abortion, so they go right out and intentionally get pregnant. I suppose they feel that they are now making up for having had that first abortion. It sounds crazy when you first think about it, but there's a sort of twisted logic to their reasoning."

I asked Dr. Holtrop how often these young pregnant girls

chose to have their babies and then give them up for adoption. "Surprisingly," he said, "that rarely happens. They either choose to have an abortion or they have the baby and keep it. Most of them seem to have a hang-up about adoption. I know it doesn't make much sense, but that's the way their minds work."

Even in the matter of birth control we are now seeing the "changed my mind" phenomenon. In the late sixties having oneself sterilized was the "in" thing to do. Arthur Godfrey bragged about his vasectomy on the radio. Young men who had fathered one or two children were crowding into doctor's offices and hospitals to have the operation. And young wives, having had two—or, at the most, three—children were requesting tubal ligations. In 1976 surgical sterilization ranked first among methods of birth control.

Most of these people, admittedly, seem to have no regrets about the decision they made in their mid- or late twenties. If they do have regrets, they don't admit to them, a situation which I think is relatively common.

Some, however, do have regrets. We are now seeing in our offices more and more women and men who want their operations reversed. Six or seven years have elapsed since their sterilizations, and changes have occurred in their lives, changes they could not have anticipated. Perhaps they are divorced and remarried to a spouse with whom they would like to have a child. Perhaps their children are now in school, and they miss having a baby around the house. Perhaps one or both of their children have died.

Unfortunately, the success rate in reversing either a vasectomy or a tubal ligation is extremely low. Most of these people must now live the remaining forty or fifty years of their lives with the results of a decision made in their twenties.

So it is imperative that the person who elects to have an abortion realize that she must live with the consequences of that procedure for the rest of her life. Often counselors—

240

physicians, nurses or sociologists—fail to sufficiently emphasize this point. The woman who is considering having an abortion should very carefully consider all the things that may or
may not happen to her during the remainder of her life, including the fact that she may never again be able to get pregnant. The abortion reversal success rate is zero.

Nor can the doctor who chooses to perform abortions have
any assurance that he will not, at a later date, regret it. Here,
from the November 28, 1974, issue of the *New England Journal of Medicine* is the first part of a statement by a physician,
Bernard N. Nathanson, M.D., who has had second thoughts.

SOUNDING BOARD
DEEPER INTO ABORTION

In early 1969 I and a group of equally concerned and
indignant citizens who had been outspoken on the subject of legalized abortion organized a political action unit
known as NARAL—then standing for National Association for Repeal of Abortion Laws, now known as the National Abortion Rights Action League. We were outspo-
kenly militant on this matter and enlisted the women's
movement and the Protestant clergy into our ranks. We
used every device available to political-action groups
such as pamphleteering, public demonstrations, exploita-
tion of the media and lobbying in the appropriate legisla-
tive chambers. In late 1969 we mounted a demonstration
outside one of the major university hospitals in New
York City that had refused to perform even therapeutic
abortions. My wife was on that picket line, and my three-
year-old son proudly carried a placard urging legalized
abortion for all. Largely as a result of the efforts of this
and a few similar groups, the monumental New York
State Abortion Statute of 1970 was passed and signed
into law by Governor Nelson Rockefeller. Our next goal

241

was to assure ourselves that low-cost, safe and humane abortions were available to all, and to that end we established the Center for Reproductive and Sexual Health, which was the first—and largest—abortion clinic in the Western world. Its record was detailed in these pages in February 1972.*

Some time ago—after a tenure of a year and a half—I resigned as director of the Center for Reproductive and Sexual Health. The Center had performed 60,000 abortions with no maternal deaths—an outstanding record of which we are proud. However, I am deeply troubled by my own increasing certainty that I had in fact presided over 60,000 deaths.

There is no longer serious doubt in my mind that human life exists within the womb from the very onset of pregnancy, despite the fact that the nature of the intrauterine life has been the subject of considerable dispute in the past. Electrocardiographic evidence of heart function has been established in embryos as early as six weeks. Electroencephalographic recordings of human brain activity have been noted in embryos at eight weeks. Our capacity to measure signs of life is daily becoming more sophisticated, and as time goes by, we will doubtless be able to isolate life signs at earlier and earlier stages in fetal development.

The Harvard Criteria for the pronouncement of death assert that if the subject is unresponsive to external stimuli (e.g., pain), if the deep reflexes are absent, if there are no spontaneous movements or respiratory efforts, if the electroencephalogram reveals no activity of the brain, one may conclude that the patient is dead. If any

*Nathanson, B. N. Ambulatory abortion experience with 26,000 cases, July 1, 1970, to August 1, 1971, *N. Engl J. Med.* 286-403-407, 1972.

or all of these criteria are absent—and the fetus does respond to pain, makes respiratory efforts, moves spontaneously and has electroencephalographic activity—life must be present.

To those who cry that nothing can be human life that cannot exist independently, I ask if the patient totally dependent for his life on treatments by the artificial kidney twice weekly is alive? Would my life be safe in this city without my eyeglasses?

Life is an interdependent phenomenon for us all. It is a continuous spectrum that begins *in utero* and ends at death—the bands of the spectrum are designated by words such as fetus, infant, child, adolescent, and adult.

We must courageously face the fact—finally—that human life of a special order is being taken. And since the vast majority of pregnancies are carried successfully to term, abortion must be seen as the interruption of a process that would otherwise have produced a citizen of the world. Denial of this reality is the crassest kind of moral evasiveness.

Dr. Nathanson's statement, the statement of a dedicated man who has done some deep soul-searching and now questions the propriety of his initial strong proabortion stand, should serve as a warning to all doctors who perform abortions. They may never regret what they are doing, but time alone will tell.

Further on in his essay Dr. Nathanson makes one more related comment worth emphasizing. "To meet the new moral challenges of the abortion decision," he says, "we may very well need specialists, some of new kinds, to serve on such a body [of counselors]—a psychohistorian, a human ecologist, a medical philosopher, an urbanologist clergyman. The counseling that such a body could offer a pregnant woman would be designed to bring the whole sweep of human experience to

243

William A. Nolen, M.D.

bear on the decision—not just the narrow partisanship of committed young women who have had abortions and who typically staff the counselor ranks of hospitals and clinics now.''

Dr. Nathanson's point is an extremely important one: the role of the counselor is really more demanding and requires more expertise than is required of the abortionist—who is, essentially, only a technician. Not to provide proper counseling for a pregnant woman—and Dr. Holtrop described the counseling services at Boston City Hospital in 1973 as "shabby at best''—would seem as much of a crime as providing incompetent medical care.

We must also, I think, realize that those who argue that a liberal abortion policy may lead to Hitlerlike extermination may be more pessimistic than is warranted, but we ignore their warnings at our peril. Here, from *Commentary*—an intellectual, predominantly Jewish, highly respected journal—is an ad that ran on a full page in several issues.

A Noose is Tightening
Around Man and Civilization

Western society has abandoned its God and is lost in a void of moral anarchy. The civilization we know is threatened by a new Dark Age.

By the turn of the century we will be confronted with abortions-by-demand-of-the-State and the death-by-decree of the sick and elderly. The planned birth, the planned lifespan, and the planned death will be upon us.

244

Let us resist this barbarous threat to man's existence, more dangerous than all the nuclear bombs.

The Non Sectarian Committee for Life
Box 1234, Mount Vernon, N.Y. 10551

It is easy to shrug these dire warnings off—to treat them as the irrational raving of antiabortion extremists—but to do so is also dangerous.

As we are now aware, moral standards are certainly not as resistant to change as most of us once believed them to be. Attitudes toward premarital and extramarital sex and toward sterilization have changed radically in the last twenty years. Those who fear that this liberalization of our attitude toward abortion may lead—logically must lead—to an acceptance of euthanasia as an answer to a burdensome aging population can certainly build an acceptable case for their position. Why, if we are willing to kill healthy, young fetuses, should we not be willing—even eager—to kill those whose lives are not only a burden on society but seem to us—if not to them—hardly worth living? The proabortionists are understandably reluctant to admit it, but the step from liberal abortion to euthanasia is a perfectly logical one. We shall have to be very, very careful that we do not take that step. If we do—and I cannot overemphasize this—life itself will lose much of its value, and society as we now know it will cease to exist.

Finally, some suggestions. Whether we are for or against abortion, we must recognize that it is now a widely accepted procedure. To talk of a constitutional amendment making abortion at any stage for any reason a crime is futile; such an amendment could never be passed. Nor do I think it should. I might remind the reader that I was a surgical resident at Bellevue from 1953 to 1955 and from 1957 to 1960. (From 1955 to

245

1957 I was in the Army.) While there I saw and helped to treat women who were admitted with hemorrhage and infections—including gas gangrene of the uterus—that resulted when abortions were self-inflicted or performed in primitive settings by untrained people. Most of those women died. I have no desire to turn the calendar back to those days.

There is, however, a middle ground between an extremely liberal "anytime" abortion philosophy and a return to the rigid antiabortion policies of the past. Compromise must be accepted by both the pro- and antiabortion segments of our society if we are ever to end this increasingly bitter battle.

I do not relish the role of pessimist or prophet of doom, but on the matter of abortion I cannot in honesty play any other. We have not only gone far enough with the liberalization of abortion laws; we have, as the Edelin case demonstrates, gone too far. We have removed too many of life's safeguards—diminished its sanctity further than we should have—and now find ourselves in a quagmire from which we must retreat. Let us consider now what we ought to do if we are to preserve what we have come to recognize as civilization.

As a first step, birth control information should be so universally available that no one will ever be able to claim it was denied them. Women are now fighting for the right to control their own bodies; with this position no reasonable person should argue. Few do. The dispute arises when the woman claims that the right to control her body and what is done to it also includes the right to control the fetus that may be growing in her uterus. This, of course, is where the proabortionists and the Right-to-Lifers part company.

That particular disagreement we will get to momentarily, but here I would like to emphasize that there is virtually no argument that a woman's right to control her body begins with the privilege of abstaining from sexual intercourse or, if she prefers, using some contraceptive method. Or insisting that

her partner do so. Some may, and do, argue that her control over pregnancy also ends with these options, but in 1978 only a wild-eyed fanatic would insist that contraception and/or abstinence are not her right.

Unfortunately we know, as I have already pointed out, that availability of contraceptive information and means are not enough to prevent unwanted pregnancies. So let us take the next step.

One reason that women, particularly young girls, are late in seeking abortions is that though they fear they are pregnant, they are hopeful they are not; witness Alice Roe's misinterpretation—or self-deception—in reporting the date of her last menstrual period to Dr. Holtrop. They practice self-denial. They don't want to be pregnant, and they hope if they wait a few more weeks, their menstrual periods will arrive and their problems will be solved.

Some women, particularly young girls, often have irregular menstrual periods. Sometimes they go several months without a menstrual period. It is easy to understand how they will hopefully attribute missed menstrual periods to irregularity, rather than accept the frightening possibility that they may be pregnant.

Most doctors who practice obstetrics have encountered at least one or two young patients who refused to admit they were pregnant till they had actually gone into labor and had to call a doctor to treat their abdominal cramps. Even I, who specialize in surgery, once had a patient come to see me because she thought she might be having an attack of appendicitis. She was, in fact, in labor.

These women could, of course, go to a doctor and have a pregnancy test done on their urine. The test is a very simple one and is about 95 percent accurate two weeks after the first missed period, i.e., when the woman is approximately four weeks pregnant. These young girls don't go to the doctor for testing either because they don't have the money to pay for a

doctor's visit or are afraid that the news of their visit to the doctor, and the reason for it, may get back to their parents.

I would suggest that the equipment needed to do a pregnancy test be put on sale in drugstores and supermarkets; now, in July 1977, it is available only at doctor's offices or in clinics concerned with pregnancy. The test, done by mixing a drop of urine with a drop of the testing solution, is so simple to do and interpret that a twelve-year-old can master it without difficulty. We should make it possible for a girl to buy this diagnostic equipment easily and inexpensively; it certainly should not cost more than two dollars, since in our clinic we figure the cost of the solutions we use to do a pregnancy test at approximately $1.20 per test. If this material were easily and cheaply available, I suspect that we would see far fewer girls making their first visits to abortion clinics with pregnancies as advanced as was Alice Roe's. In fact, if this equipment had been accessible to Alice Roe, I doubt that there would ever have been an Edelin case.

It can be argued that counseling centers, where free or almost free pregnancy tests can be done, are already available. But they are not as ubiquitous as supermarkets or drugstores. And girls or women who visit them may have to register or in some other way identify themselves. The person who buys a pregnancy testing kit in a supermarket can preserve her anonymity.

As to the matter of financing abortions, a controversial subject it is perhaps cowardly to avoid, I think that here, too, compromise may be the only acceptable solution.

Pregnancy is not, like cancer, a condition that a person acquires for reasons she does not understand or cannot avoid, except, perhaps, the first time, or in those extremely rare cases where the pregnancy is a result of rape or incest or seriously threatens the life or health of the mother.

Since the government will pay the medical expenses of the indigent person who suffers a heart attack, is afflicted with

cancer or acquires pneumonia, it seems reasonable that the government pay for an abortion that results from rape or from ignorance of methods of birth control.

But since ignorance of birth control measures should certainly be "cured" at the same time the abortion is performed, any subsequent pregnancies should be the financial responsibility of the patient who becomes pregnant—again, excepting pregnancies that result from rape or incest.

Such a policy would place the responsibility for avoiding pregnancy where it belongs: on the individual. Already, for example, by making abortions inexpensively and readily available in college health clinics, we have, as a society, encouraged young people to look upon abortion as "just another perfectly acceptable method of birth control," as one college student told me. We have encouraged them to adopt an attitude that reduces the value of life.

If we add a financial penalty to the moral stigma of abortion—a moral stigma that is rapidly diminishing—we may in part reverse the casual attitude toward abortion that is becoming so prevalent, particularly among the young.

Next—and I suspect this is the suggestion which will run into the most opposition from the more radical proponents of women's rights—I believe we must, in fairness to the fetus, demand that the woman who decides she wants an abortion make that decision before the twentieth week of pregnancy. In *Roe* v. *Wade* the Supreme Court permitted but did not compel states to protect the rights of fetuses *in utero* only in the third trimester, i.e., after the twenty-fourth week of pregnancy. Presumably they chose to allow the states to limit abortion only in the third trimester because in 1973 it was virtually impossible for a baby to survive if it were born before the twenty-eighth week. Using the twenty-fourth week as the cutoff point would seem to have allowed a margin of error of four weeks. But, as the Edelin case demonstrated only too well, this margin is not adequate.

249

William A. Nolen, M.D.

In the five years since *Roe* v. *Wade* became law, survival rates for infants weighing 800–1000 grams—infants of approximately twenty-seven or twenty-eight weeks of gestation—have soared to 60 percent. The increased salvage rate is generally attributed to a change in physician attitude. Physicians felt in 1973 that these tiny infants couldn't survive, so little was done to help them. We then discovered that if we worked with these children, utilizing our most sophisticated life-support systems, they could and did live. However, because of the immaturity of their lungs, no infants of less than twenty-four weeks gestation have survived. (Possibly this will change, and if so, the law may have to be changed. At the moment survival for more than a very few minutes, at less than twenty-four weeks, is impossible and seems likely to remain that way.)

As the Edelin case showed, it is impossible to determine duration of pregnancy with complete accuracy. Fetuses of twenty-four weeks' maturity may, in some instances, be able to survive outside the uterus. So let us be even safer than *Roe* v. *Wade* sought to make us. Let us protect the fetus after twenty weeks of gestation, not by state law but by national law. The fetus in New York should have the same chance to live as the fetus in Massachusetts.

Let us also make it compulsory to have at least two doctors agree that the fetus is not more than twenty weeks old. To leave the decision as to fetal age and, consequently, viability to any one doctor not only puts too great a burden on the doctor—legally and morally—but also leaves the door open for those few physicians who are willing to abort even an obviously viable fetus in order to cultivate an abortionist practice. We don't need those physicians in our society.

Is it unfair to reduce the time when a woman may have abortion on demand from twenty-four to twenty weeks? I think not. To reduce the woman's option by one month, in or-

der that we may avoid a problem such as that which arose in the Edelin case, does not seem unreasonable. We will only be asking women to give up four of the twenty-four weeks they now have in which to choose or not choose an abortion, hardly a significant sacrifice when weighed against the possibility that it may afford an infant seventy or more years of life. (The doctor that cannot estimate the length of gestation within four weeks has no business practicing obstetrics at all.)

Quickening—fetal movement—is felt between the sixteenth and eighteenth week. The woman who does not realize she is pregnant by the time she reaches twenty weeks probably won't realize it till she gives birth to the baby. Asking her to decide for or against abortion by the twentieth week hardly seems unreasonable. (Exceptions could be made in the case of the girl who is so young or so mentally retarded that she does not realize she is pregnant till someone else tells her. One might also except the woman who does not learn till the twenty-first week that the fetus she is carrying is mentally or physically defective; diagnostic amniocentesis (a procedure in which a syringe is used to withdraw a sample of amniotic fluid) can be done fourteen to sixteen weeks after the last menstrual period, but it may take two to five weeks to properly grow and study the cells and detect any abnormality of the fetus. But if these exceptions are made—and I am not sure that in every case they should be; no one has ever proven that having a baby is any more damaging to a young girl's psyche than having an abortion—the burden of deciding on the exception should be made by the woman, the doctor and a consultant following a prescribed legal format.

The consultant might be sort of an abortion ombudsperson, like the one described by Dr. Nathanson in the quote on page 243: a person who will review the economic, political, social, religious and psychological ramifications of abortion as well as the mother's other options.

However, exceptions to the general rule that abortions should not be permitted after twenty weeks should not be so easily arranged that they become the rule.

Finally, in any abortion when there is even an extremely remote chance that a live birth will result—that is, in all abortions done by hysterotomy or saline amniocentesis (obviously, in an abortion done by D&C the fetus is removed in pieces, and no baby ever exists)—the baby should be given every reasonable aid to help it live. If the baby is removed at sixteen weeks by hysterotomy, even though the chance that it will survive is virtually nil, some responsible person—doctor or nurse—should do what he or she can to grant the baby that chance. At the very least the child should be checked thoroughly for any signs of life. If they are present, no matter how weak, the child should be put in an incubator; its mouth and trachea should be cleaned of mucus, and it should be stimulated by medications or physical methods in an honest attempt to help it breathe. It may gasp for 10 seconds—two minutes—or one hour—but for however brief or long a time it shows any sign of life, it should be treated with the care that we give to fully developed human beings. The routine followed by Dr. Edelin in the Alice Roe case—a hand on the infant's chest for five seconds followed by disposal—should be deemed unequivocally unacceptable.

If the Edelin case teaches us anything, it is that life—however fragile—is precious, and we have an obligation to nurture it with all the skill and compassion at our command. To do less is to cheapen life and to reduce its value.

We have only to consider the atrocities of which "civilized" people have been guilty in the last fifty years to realize that we are not as incapable of barbaric behavior as we would like to believe. Casual acceptance of abortion as an answer to social problems could, if we are not careful, be the first step down a path that leads to the end of civilization as we know it.

252

Afterword

As this book goes to press (February 1978), the body of Baby Boy Roe, born on October 3, 1973, remains in a jar on the shelf in the Suffolk County Medical Examiner's morgue. No one will sign his death certificate, so he cannot legally be buried.

scholar

\riminichs tremendous